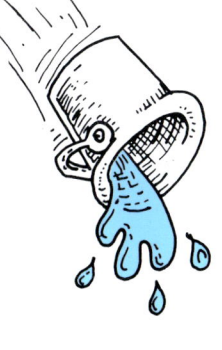

Much Ado About Something

Written by Andrew Smith

Aided and abetted by Chris Allen, Terry Clutterham, Malcolm Ingham, Graeme Hatton and Sarah Smith.

Contents

PAGE	
3	Introduction
4	Terrific Top Tips for Dynamic Drama
6	The Usurper .... Who is Jesus?
8	The Pet .... Witnessing
10	The Assembly .... Prejudice
12	Ridiculous Routes .... The uniqueness of Christ
14	Spot the Brain Cell .... Lying
16	The Debtors .... Forgiveness
18	Caiaphas's Catastrophic Caper .... The Resurrection
20	Playing Tonight .... Worship
22	It's a Fair Cop .... Sin and forgiveness
24	The Kept Promise .... God's promises
26	What Would You do? .... Persecution
28	Lord Wormington Squirrel and his Faithful Butler, Boote .... Obedience
30	Empty-handed .... Death
32	Innocent .... Why did Jesus die?
34	Beyond the Game .... The nature of God
36	Be Prepared .... Holy living
38	All Change .... Zacchaeus
40	An Eye for an Eye .... Revenge
42	All or Nothing .... Confession
44	The Exhibition .... Criticism
46	Other resources from Pathfinders
48	Bible Index

Introduction

Eleven to fourteen year olds often fall between churches' children's groups and their youth groups, but they need resources and activities to suit them, so that they can learn about God and grow in their Christian lives. Young teenagers like things that happen, things that are entertaining and things that involve the leaders getting water thrown at them! *Much Ado About Something* contains all these and more. Contained within the pages of this glossy and attractive book are twenty tried and tested sketches for you to use with your eleven to fourteen year olds group. Some are funny, a few are serious-ish, most are fairly silly. But they all help teach young teenagers about the Bible and about our relationship with God.

The sketches would work in a variety of settings: a weekly youth group, a family service, a mission or a school assembly. They are all written with the aim of making them easy to learn, easy to perform and short. They could all be performed equally well by leaders, or by members of the group who see themselves as budding actors.

TRAILER

If you wish to perform them on their own, or perform a number of them at one event, then each sketch comes with a trailer. This is a short sentence you can use after the sketch to help the young people think about the issues that have been raised.

WORKSHOP

These are suggestions for how you can use the sketch in a group meeting. Each sketch can be used to illustrate a different point. There is reference made to the relevant Bible passages and, where appropriate, discussion starters you can use with your group. The sketches were originally written to fit in with a specific theme for a youth group session, and this has been reflected in the titles and explanations. However, if you think you can teach another point just as well from the sketch, go ahead. Use them how, when and where you like.

DIRECTOR'S TIPS

These are to help you understand what crazy ideas I had in mind when I wrote the sketch. They also give you hints and tips on how to perform it to the best of your ability.

Throughout the book I've referred to performers, audiences and stages. Don't worry, I'm not expecting you to hire the local theatre and put on an evening's entertainment of Pathfinder sketches – although it would be great if you did! Anybody playing any of the parts in any sketch counts as a performer, anybody watching counts as audience and wherever you do the sketch counts as a stage. I know it sounds all very dramatic and grand, but I had to call them something and performer, audience and stage seemed as good as anything!

Most the sketches in *Much Ado About Something* have come from other resources published for Pathfinders. Since they were first published, some of them have had a re-write. This has been done to make the sketches even better than they were originally — I hope it works!

Ten Terrific Top Tips for Dynamic Drama

1. **Rehearse**
2. **Rehearse**
3. **Rehearse**
4. **Rehearse**
5. **Rehearse**

NB. If you are doing improvisation, you may omit number 3.

Having mastered those rules, here are one or two others that will help you in your quest to entertain, amuse and teach through drama.

6 Be Visual

Whatever you're doing, for however many people, your sketch will be greatly enhanced if people can see what you are doing. Even the keenest teenager will soon lose interest if the sketch they are 'watching' is more suited to the radio.

So check the space where you will be performing. If you can get up on a stage, get up there. If, like most of us, you don't possess a handy stage, make sure your audience is sitting down and try and perform as much of the sketch as possible standing up or hanging from the rafters.

Make your performers visually interesting as well. You don't need major costumes and make-up for every sketch but suggestions of costumes like hats, scarves or coats all add to the performance. Small props like umbrellas and briefcases are also easy to collect and make the sketch more visual. This might seem like a lot of bother for a short sketch in front of a small group. But it's worth it, believe me! If you perform sketches regularly, build up a store of costumes and props. You can get some great stuff very cheaply if you look round at jumble sales, car boot sales and charity shops.

Use your body and facial expressions to be visual as well. When you rehearse the sketches, note all the different emotions that your character needs to feel. Think about how you are going to show them. Obviously the easiest place to start is with your face, if the character is happy you can smile. But what is the rest of your body doing? What do you do with your arms if you are happy? How do you stand or walk? When you've thought through all these things practise them, making sure all your movements and expressions can be seen. They will need to be much bigger and stronger than normal if all the audience is going to see what you are doing.

7 Be Audible

Your audience will love you far more if they can hear what you are going on about in your performance. What's more, they might even learn something! Being clear and audible is not something that comes naturally to most people, so you'll probably have to practise this bit. Firstly, make sure you've learnt the lines properly, then you can stop worrying about trying to remember them and can concentrate on delivering them well.

Think through how you are going to express your character by the tone of your voice. How can you vary the pitch, or pace of what you are saying? If you have no variety in your voice, it becomes monotonous and boring. It also become harder to understand. The audience will be listening as much to the tone of your voice, as to what you are saying.

Practise your sketch where you are going to perform it. Have someone sit a long way from you and shout 'Pardon?' every time they can't hear you. This is very annoying, but it highlights just how unclear we often are. You will want to work not just on being loud enough, but also being slow enough and clear enough in your pronunciation. Often your speech will sound really slow, loud and silly when it is audible to anybody else, but it is important that your audience can hear your lovely voice. If the sketch needs to move fast, don't just start talking more quickly. The key is to come in on cue really fast. So as the person before you finishes their line, you are already starting yours. This gives the impression of people talking really quickly, even if the lines are still slow enough to hear.

Work really hard on those bits where there is something happening in the sketch that will drown out the sound: for example, people running whilst talking, speaking into a telephone, having water thrown at them during a speech and so on.

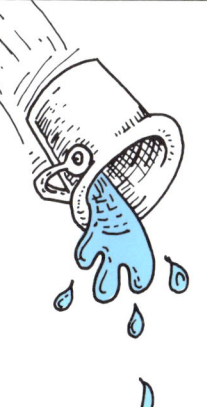

8 Be Active

Drama should be dramatic. It stands to reason really, but sadly much of it isn't. Young teenagers are going to enjoy and remember your performance much more if there is some action in it somewhere. This doesn't have to be people falling over and throwing things at each other, although it's good if they do! Have people moving around, standing, sitting, storming off. If you have a lot of action in a sketch, you can highlight a significant moment by being still. Stillness needn't be freezing in dramatic positions, but being still physically and emotionally.

If your acting space is so small you really can't do any of these things, make sure there is action in the speech. Whether it is someone getting really angry, or being genuinely grief-stricken. Get some action in there somewhere. Like stillness in the middle of action, a pause in the dialogue can heighten drama. In the middle of a loud fast-moving sketch, a long pause will have tremendous impact. Don't forget, there is a difference between pausing and stopping to remember your lines. During a pause the actors are still performing, and the audience should be able to see what they are thinking.

9 Be Relevant

Always remember who your audience are. The sketches in this book have been written for young teenagers. They might work if you choose to perform them at the Over 80s club, but I can't guarantee it! Remember that it's young teenagers who will be your main audience, so it's their humour and understanding you want to appeal to. If you are not sure what appeals to young teenagers, find out. Watch some of their programmes, read their magazines or better still ask some of them! Don't forget it's to them you are performing, so you may not find the sketches particularly inspiring or funny, but hopefully the young teenagers will.

Feel free with any of the sketches to adapt the characters and locations to fit your situation. So you can change the gender of any of the characters to fit with your ratio of male to female performers. Where places are mentioned you can make them local to you, and where any famous people or programmes are mentioned you can swap them with current favourites.

10 Be Enthusiastic

You might feel embarrassed at having to perform in some of the sketches in this book, but that's a sacrifice we all have to make. However, if you perform the sketch looking embarrassed the young people will either laugh themselves silly at your expense or will just get bored and stop watching. So go for it in a big way!

Remember, you may find it hard to have the confidence to do all this, but if you want 11s-14s to perform in front of their peers, they will often find it even harder than you do. Always make sure they are happy to perform the sketch, and work hard at building up their own self-confidence.

All the sketches in this book can be performed in under four minutes, so give it your all for those few minutes. Your enthusiasm will be infectious. The young people will respond to your enthusiasm and will enjoy the sketch much more. A good rule to remember: the smaller the audience, the more enthusiastic you need to be to carry them with you through the sketch.

The Usurper

KING EGBERT CORNICHE XXXIII — A well meaning king.
QUEEN CORNICHE — His wife.
DUKE MARMADUKE OF MALMSBURY — The king's royal adviser.
CASPAR CUSPINCE — A villain who's trying to depose the king.

(The KING and QUEEN are sitting on thrones. The DUKE is standing beside the KING.)
KING: *(Shouting regally)* Call the next subject!
QUEEN: Don't shout, dearie!
KING: *(Still shouting)* Pardon?
QUEEN: Don't shout, dearie. You know it brings on one of my heads.
KING: *(Aside)* Yes, well, any would be better than that one!
QUEEN: Pardon?
KING: Nothing, sweetness. *(Whispering deliberately to the DUKE)* Could you call the next subject?
DUKE: Yes, your Superiorness. *(He looks at a piece of paper.)*
KING: *(To the QUEEN)* I do like it when he calls me that. It adds a certain regality to everything.
DUKE: The next subject will beeeee ... Geography!
KING: *(Clipping him round the ear)* Oh ha, ha, ha! Very witty. Not *that* sort of subject! Now stop telling jokes and get on with it. Or perhaps you would like to be the court jester. Actually I think a little hat with bells would quite suit you.
DUKE: No, no, your Munificence. Not the hat with the bells on, your Graciousness. I was merely trying to put some life into this otherwise dying sketch, your Excellency.
KING: OK. Get on with it!
DUKE: Yes, your Wonderfulness. The next subject is crafty Caspar Cuspince, wanted for treachery, treason and tree-pinching.
(CASPAR enters as if he has been thrown in. He kneels in front of the KING and QUEEN.)
KING: So, Cooper ...
DUKE: Caspar!
KING: Eh? Oh, yes. So, Caspar, we have you at last!
CASPAR: *(Standing up)* You may have me now, but I shall soon be free, Egg Head!
KING: Egg Head? How dare you call me Egg Head! It's Egbert Corniche the 33rd to you.
QUEEN: Who is this horrible man, Eggypoos?
KING: Don't call me Eggypoos in front of the subjects, dear. He's Kevin Cuprinol – some rogue or other.
CASPAR: Actually, Queenie, I'm Caspar Cuspince. And soon I shall be king instead of this Eggypoos.
DUKE: How dare you call his Marvellousness 'Eggypoos'? Say sorry at once!
CASPAR: Oh yeah? And who are *you?*
DUKE: I'm Duke Marmaduke of Malmsbury, adviser to his Kingliness King Egbert Corniche the 33rd.
CASPAR: *(Pushing him over)* Creep!
KING: *(Standing and shouting)* Now look here, Cleethorpes!
CASPAR: Caspar!
KING: Oh, all right, Caspar. What is it you want, you snivelling knave?
CASPAR: I want your throne, Bertie.
KING: *(Losing all control)* Don't call me Bertie! *(He sits.)*
QUEEN: Anyway, don't be so silly. If you have the throne, where will dear Eggy Weggy sit?
CASPAR: Not the chair — the throne! I want to be king!
QUEEN: Oh, *that!* Well, why didn't you say? We've been wanting to give up for a long time, haven't we, dear? All this sitting around being called silly names — what sort of a job's that, eh? Look, you just give us time to get packed and then you can take over. How's that?
CASPAR: But, but, but ...
KING: Yes, that's right, Jasper. You can take all this!
CASPAR: *(Totally exasperated)* It's Caspar!
KING: Yes, it probably is, Cuthbert.
(The KING and QUEEN exit quite happily.)
CASPAR: Ha, it's all mine now! *(He sits on the throne.)*
Now, Marmy Babes, start treating me like the king, or it's off with your head!
DUKE: Oh, shut up, you wally! *(He runs off.)*
CASPAR: Hey, come back! Come here, all of you! Come and call me 'King'! Come and call me 'Your Majesty'!
(He exits.) Call me 'Your Excellence'! Someone call me 'Your Highness'...

Who is Jesus?

TRAILER

What we call people shows what we think of them. What do you call Jesus?

WORKSHOP

All the characters in the sketch called the King different things. Ask the group to list who called him what. The names they called him reflected their attitude to him and their relationship with him. It also reflected their response to the things he said. In the sketch the King had many names that people used to address him. Jesus also has many names. Our use of them reflects our attitude to him. One of the names people use most often is 'Lord'. Look at **Matthew 7:21**. Here Jesus is saying that lots of people call him Lord, but calling him that isn't enough on its own. We also need to obey him.

If you want to help the group spot all the names that people call the King (there are thirteen different names, I think), why not video yourselves acting out the sketch before the meeting and then show the video to the group. This means they can watch it once just for fun, then you can replay it to count all the names.

Using video is a good way of presenting drama in a different way, which is often highly entertaining. It also enables you to use performers who might not be able to be at your group meeting.

DIRECTOR'S TIPS

☞ Contrast the King and Caspar Cuspince. When they first meet Caspar wants to dominate and be in control. Gradually the roles change and by the time the King exits he does so with dignity. Caspar is left, rather pathetically demanding that people call him names.

☞ Use this sketch as a lively start to a group session and keep the pace of it fast and furious.

☞ The characters can be as daft as you like. Try to give them appropriate costumes. If they end up looking like pantomime characters, so much the better.

The Pet

ALEX — A non-Christian trying to take his pet for a walk.
MICHAEL — A rather pious Christian.

(You need to have 'wing space' for this sketch, a screen at the side of the stage which the audience can't see behind. ALEX is on stage holding one end of a long piece of rope. On the other end of the rope, unseen in the wings, is Florence, a wild animal. Have someone in the wings holding the rope and jerking it as if there is a large wild beast attached. ALEX is struggling to maintain control.)

ALEX: *(Shouting at Florence)* Come on girl, walkies! That's right, heel! No! Will you please just walkies! *(MICHAEL enters from the other side of the stage.)* Michael! Just the person I wanted to see.

MICHAEL: *(Looking nervously off stage at Florence)* Er, hi Alex! How can I help?

ALEX: It's my pet, Florence. I'm trying to take her for a walk. You couldn't give us a hand, could you?

MICHAEL: Unfortunately I've only got two, and I'm using them both at the moment.

ALEX: Ha, ha, very witty – but could you please help me with Florence? Before she gets out of control.

MICHAEL: Well I could, but what sort of pet is Florence?

ALEX: A very big one.

MICHAEL: I can see that. But a very big what?

ALEX: A very big, long haired, lesser-spotted, Mongolian, angry one. That's what.

MICHAEL: I see. Look, I'll see what I can do. *(He looks nervously at Florence, then walks to the opposite side of the stage and kneels down.)*

ALEX: Thanks...er, what are you doing?

MICHAEL: I'm praying that God will help you control Florence, of course.

ALEX: What?

MICHAEL: You carry on and I'll pray that God'll give you the strength to take Florence for a walk and the money to pay for all the damage she's done.

ALEX: Well, if you say so.

(MICHAEL prays silently for about fifteen seconds, with his lips moving and gesticulating with his hands. While he is praying ALEX is dragged off stage by Florence. As he goes he gestures wildly for MICHAEL to help.)

MICHAEL: *(Loudly)* Aaa-men. Right, well, there you go Alex. Alex? Alex?

ALEX: *(Re-enters pulling very hard and looking dishevelled)* Well thanks, fat lot of use you are.

MICHAEL: Would you like me to pray again?

ALEX: No! Just grab hold of this rope.

MICHAEL: *(MICHAEL does not grab hold of the rope, but faces the audience and gets very holy. As the speech progresses, ALEX manages to get to MICHAEL and give him the rope. MICHAEL takes hold without realizing. He should take the rope just before he is whisked off stage.)* You know, I'm glad you've given me this opportunity to help you. It's not often that as a Christian you get the chance to help your friend who's in need, and it's a great privilege to know that I'm able to serve the Lord by helping a friend. And it's great to know that you feel able to ask me to help, knowing it will bring a willing response. Throughout my life I have always said that it is in the little things that we are able to live out our Christian faith by being there when the need arises. By demonstrating love in action, by speaking boldly, by being courageous, by, by... *(At this point MICHAEL is whisked off stage, making it look as if Florence has just run off.)*

ALEX: *(Looking off stage at MICHAEL and waving)* Bye, bye! *(He brushes the dust of his hands, and exits in the other direction.)*

Witnessing

TRAILER

Michael wanted Alex to know about Jesus. But what would you have done?

WORKSHOP

Michael wanted Alex to know about Jesus. Michael certainly spoke about being a Christian, but did the message get across? Ask the group members to think of one person who has shown them what Jesus is like. How did they show that?

Look at **Acts 16:16-34**. Get the group to pin-point the times and ways that Paul and Silas were witnessing. Highlight both their actions and what they said to the jailer. Ask the group to imagine what the other prisoners must have thought and said about Paul and Silas. We tell others about our faith, not only by what we say, but also by what we do and how we do it.

DIRECTOR'S TIPS

☞ Bring out the humour of this sketch by having Alex work hard at making it look as though he is fighting to stay on stage. Practise by pulling a piece of rope with someone pulling against you. Look at the way you use your whole body to pull on the rope. Having done that, try and copy those same movements in the sketch. Add some appropriate facial expressions and grunting and groaning noises, and you'll soon have all the audience believing that Florence is about to dash off with you.

☞ Michael needs to be equally excessive when he's praying. He should be really wrestling in prayer, spiritually and physically, and completely oblivious to everything else that is going on.

☞ Set the scene by having Alex struggle with Florence for about fifteen seconds before he says anything.

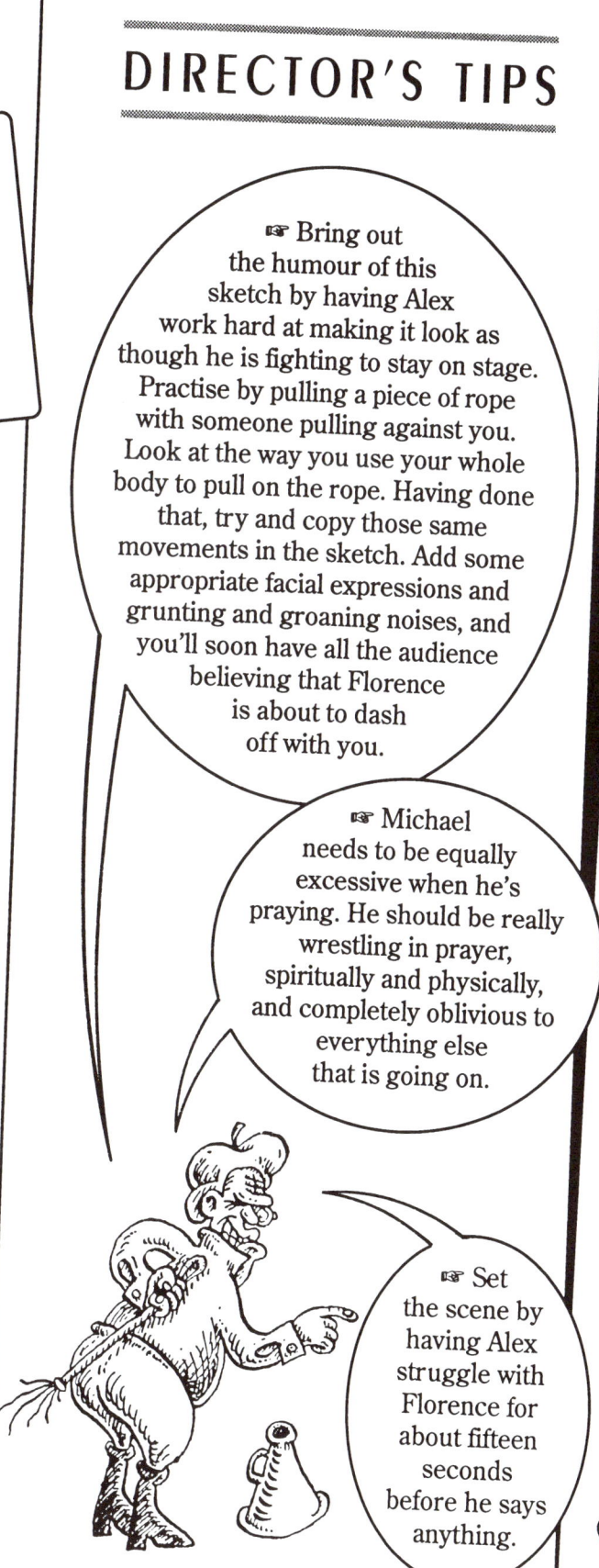

9

The Assembly

MISS WILKINSON — who dislikes Malcolm.
MALCOLM — an innocent victim.
HEADTEACHER — a fair person.

(*At the start of the sketch MALCOLM is sitting in with the rest of the group. Enter MISS WILKINSON.*)

MISS WILKINSON: Good morning everybody.

PUPILS: (*This will only be MALCOLM and any other leaders.*) Good morning Miss.

MISS WILKINSON: Well that wasn't a very good start. Let's try again, good morning everybody.

PUPILS: Good morning Miss.

MISS WILKINSON: Now then, before we start this morning's assembly, I have one or two things to say regarding the rather unfortunate incident involving the school cat and a vat of cold custard. You will be pleased to hear that the vet has said that the cat will be all right, but he is now terrified of anything yellow. Now, all the staff and myself are determined to find and punish the culprits and in fact we, or at least I, have a fairly good idea who is to blame, don't we Malcolm?

MALCOLM: Pardon?

MISS WILKINSON: Don't answer me back, boy. Now come out to the front here. (*MALCOLM goes up to the front and turns to face the group.*) Go and stand in the corner with your face to the wall. None of us wants to look at you.

MALCOLM: (*Not moving*) But I haven't done anything.

MISS WILKINSON: Such nonsense! You own a Latvian Pekinese short-haired show dog, don't you?

MALCOLM: Well, yes but...

MISS WILKINSON: Well there you are, an obvious cat hater, and as the local secretary of the Feline Friendly Fellowship I can tell you that we take a pretty tough line against your sort. Now go and stand in the corner. (*MALCOLM goes and stands in the corner with his face to the wall. MISS WILKINSON then turns her attention to the rest of the group.*) Now then boys and girls, we've had a letter from the Director of Shortleat Safari park inviting us to go and have a VIP trip round the park. We'll be able to help feed all the animals and go behind the scenes to see what life's really like at a Safari Park. We will be going next Thursday, although there'll be a certain animal hater who'll be staying behind to do some extra work. (*MISS WILKINSON glares at MALCOLM.*) Now I know that you all love animals and would never do anything as cruel as this boy has done, so I don't want any of you feeling sorry for Malcolm or buying him gifts from Shortleat. Just keep thinking about how the school cat must have felt in all that cold custard. I want you all to leave Malcolm well alone and let him know that his sort aren't wanted round here. OK — now that's all for this morning... (*The HEADTEACHER enters.*)

HEADTEACHER: Ah Miss Wilkinson, I knew you'd be particularly anxious to hear that the police have just arrested the gang who tortured the school cat. Now what's young Malcolm doing up here? Of course, you must be telling the school how his project won our trip to Shortleat. Well done, Malcolm. OK Miss Wilkinson, you may dismiss the school. (*The HEADTEACHER exits.*)

MISS WILKINSON: (*To MALCOLM, very vindictively*) So, you won the prize did you? Think you have helped the school by your dog-loving antics, do you? Well we don't want your kind of help, Malcolm. This school has never taken charity from cat haters of any kind. (*To the pupils*) I am sad to say, boys and girls, that our trip to Shortleat Safari Park and cat haters' paradise... has been cancelled. (*She storms off and MALCOLM returns to his seat.*)

Prejudice

TRAILER

We pick on some people for no good reason. For Miss Wilkinson it was dog owners. Are you sure you're not prejudiced?

WORKSHOP

Ask the group members if any of them has ever experienced blind prejudice against them or someone else. Malcolm was clearly being picked on by Miss Wilkinson. There was no basis for this prejudice other than the fact that Malcolm owned a dog. There were certain facts about people in Jesus' day that were used against them as an excuse for prejudice. Some were Samaritans; some were lepers; about half were women; even more were poor. Look at **Luke 17:11-19**. The man at the centre of this passage is an outsider on two accounts. He was both a leper and a Samaritan. But the passage shows how Jesus loves all, even those considered outsiders. Point out to the group that just as Jesus loved the outsider, we should do the same.

Ask the group the following questions:

Who are the outsiders in today's society?

What would Jesus' reaction be to them if he were on earth now?

What should our reaction be to them?

DIRECTOR'S TIPS

☞ The sketch takes the form of an assembly and needs to be introduced by a leader announcing, 'And now it's time for this morning's assembly.'

☞ When Miss Wilkinson is telling Malcolm off she can become completely furious, but then extremely kind and generous towards the rest of the group.

☞ Brief the other leaders to join in and co-operate where necessary, but keep the sketch a secret from everyone else.

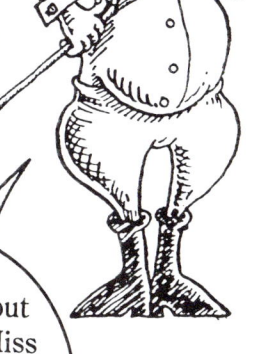

☞ Throughout the sketch, Miss Wilkinson addresses the audience as if they are the pupils.

Ridiculous Routes

NIGEL — A rather lost person.
GERSHWIN — Plays a variety of rather unhelpful people.
RORY — A jolly helpful chap.

(*NIGEL enters looking lost. Enter GERSHWIN.*)

GERSHWIN: (*A rather snooty character*) I say, are you lost?

NIGEL: No, I'm Nigel.

GERSHWIN: Oh well, can I offer my navigational expertise to you in any way?

NIGEL: Well, I'd prefer it if you could tell me how to get to the village.

GERSHWIN: Oh, is that all? Well, that's no problem, old bean. What you want to do is toddle on down to Biffy's place, when you get there head on round till you arrive at old Stinker's home — now he's a rummy cove if ever there was. After strolling along there for a brisk moment or two, cut across Freddy's orchard and before you know it you'll be strolling through the village as perky as a pig in a poke.

NIGEL: (*Looking very lost.*) Uh huh, and is that all?

GERSHWIN: Yep, it's as easy as...well something that's frightfully easy. Toodle pip, old chap! (*He exits.*)

NIGEL: Um yeah, toodle thingy. (*He looks around, lost.*) What was all that rubbish about? Toddle down to Stinker's orchard, then biff up Freddy? What a waste of time.

(*Enter GERSHWIN in a different disguise.*)

GERSHWIN: (*As a country yokel*) 'Ere, are you lost?

NIGEL: No, I'm Nigel.

GERSHWIN: Aaarr. What would you be doing 'ere then, Mr Nigel?

NIGEL: I'm trying to get to the village.

GERSHWIN: Aaarr.

NIGEL: Do you know the way to the village?

GERSHWIN: Aaarr.

NIGEL: Have I seen you somewhere before?

GERSHWIN: Naarr.

NIGEL: Will you stop saying 'aaarr'!

GERSHWIN: Aaarr (*pause*). The village, you say?

NIGEL: Aaarr...I mean yes, the village.

GERSHWIN: Aaarr (*pause*). Well if I were you, I'd nip right sharpish across them there fields, till yer comes to the old beech tree, then follow the hawthorn till ye sees the crow's nest in the tall oak. Follow the stream as far as ye can, then where the reeds are growing, cut through the wood till ye sees the church spire. Then ye'll be in the village. (*He exits.*)

NIGEL: (*Calling after him*) Thanks. You were about as much help as that last person. Someone round here must know the way to this village!

(*Enter GERSHWIN dressed normally.*)

GERSHWIN: Are you lost?

NIGEL: No, I'm Nigel. But do you know the way to the village?

GERSHWIN: Yes, it's over there. (*He points vaguely and exits.*)

NIGEL: Yeah, well that was really helpful. Thanks a lot.

(*Enter RORY*)

RORY: Are you lost?

NIGEL: No, I'm...Oh forget it — no one's laughed. Yes I am lost. Do you know how to get to the village?

RORY: Yes, it's easy. Why don't you come with me. I'm going that way myself. (*They exit.*)

The Uniqueness of Christ

TRAILER

Lots of people have tried to tell us how to get to heaven. Jesus said, 'I am the way, come with me.'

WORKSHOP

Throughout the sketch all Gershwin could offer was instructions on how to get to the village. He told Nigel the way, but then left him to get there on his own. Rory, on the other hand, actually went to the village with Nigel.

Read **John 14:6**. Jesus didn't say to Thomas, 'I know the way', or 'Go that way'. What made Jesus' claim so remarkable and unique was that he said, 'I am the way'. Just like Rory showed Nigel the way to the village by going with him, Jesus takes us to enjoy the friendship and help of God. Jesus is the only way to reach right to God.

DIRECTOR'S TIPS

☞ Gershwin needs to be able to change character very quickly. Have a few hats ready for him to change between each person. He could also put on exaggerated accents for each character.

☞ Nigel needs to become more and more exasperated and angry as the sketch goes on until, finally, Rory is able to help him.

Spot the Brain Cell

QUESTION MASTER — Surname needs to be a Christian name plus 'son' (for example, Peter Peterson).
CONTESTANT
KNUCKLES and **BRUISER** — Two thugs.

(*The scene is a Mastermind-type quiz.*)

QM:	Good evening and welcome to *Spot the Brain Cell*, and please give a big hand to our first contestant. (*Contestant enters looking nervous and sits on chair.*) Your name please?
CONTESTANT:	Betty Frillsop. (*This will need to be Norris Bilgewater if the contestant is female.*)
QM:	And your chosen subject?
CONTESTANT:	Telling the truth.
QM:	Well, you have one minute to answer questions on lying. Starting...now. (*The next part should be performed very quickly.*) Who is the Archbishop of Canterbury?
CONTESTANT:	I am.
QM:	Correct. Where is the Channel Tunnel?
CONTESTANT:	Birmingham.
QM:	Correct. What is the square root of 37?
CONTESTANT:	A cheese and marmalade sandwich.
QM:	Correct. What is the capital of Hawaii?
CONTESTANT:	A small blue cat.
QM:	Correct. Who was the King of Denmark in 1437?
CONTESTANT:	Liverpool Football Club.
QM:	Correct. What do you call the gap between two mountains?
CONTESTANT:	Er...pass.
QM:	No, I'm sorry, that is the true answer. The answer we were looking for was halibut. Which planet is on the edge of the Solar System?
CONTESTANT:	Bognor Regis.
QM:	Correct. (*They return to normal speed at this point.*) And that means that you have scored six points. As you know that means that you have the chance to win today's star prize of a world cruise plus £10,000 spending money. To win this fabulous prize all you have to do is answer the following question truthfully. Do you want this prize?
CONTESTANT:	Yes, I do.
QM:	(*With great enthusiasm*) Then the prize is yours. You will be leaving straight after the show.
CONTESTANT:	But I don't want to go!
QM:	What?
CONTESTANT:	I don't want to go...I hate travelling...boats make me feel sick...and I'll miss the Cup Final if I go now.
QM:	Then why did you say 'yes'?
CONTESTANT:	I was lying...that's why I'm here...I'm a great liar.
QM:	Indeed you are, (*the Question Master becomes decidedly determined and menacing*) which is why I don't believe you now. So you *will* go on the cruise, and to help you on your way the lovely Knuckles and Bruiser are here to see you off. (*Two thugs enter and manhandle the CONTESTANT off. The CONTESTANT should resist as much as possible.*) Well that's all for tonight's show. We'll see you next week: same time, same channel for another exciting edition of *Spot the Brain Cell*.
CONTESTANT:	(*Off stage and full of pleading*) But I really don't want to go!

Lying

TRAILER

You can fool some of the people all of the time. And all of the people some of the time. But you can't fool God any of the time. Lying won't do you any good.

WORKSHOP

Discuss what is the worst thing about telling lies. When we start lying we find it hard to stop. We end up living a lie, just like the contestant had to go along with his lies and ended up having to go on the cruise. Eventually all we do is continually try to deceive other people and ourselves.

In **James 5:19**, James is talking about a godly way of living, rather than about telling the truth in particular. The 'truth' James mentions is the truth of the Gospel and the way that we should live according to it. We have a responsibility to encourage each other to live in a manner that is worthy of being a follower of Jesus.

DIRECTOR'S TIPS

☞ Make sure that the Question Master and contestant can be seen by the audience. The best way to do this is have them sitting at a slight angle to each other. For example:

Audience

☞ Set the scene by singing the theme tune to *Mastermind*. (It sort of goes 'Dum dum dum dum... dee dum'.)

☞ Make sure the sketch starts and ends in a very slow and controlled way. The middle section, when the questions are being put, should be as fast and as clear as possible.

☞ The Question Master needs to become decidedly menacing throughout the final section. It should be very clear that the contestant genuinely doesn't want to go, but is not going to be able to get out of it.

The Debtors

A SHOP MANAGER
A SHOP ASSISTANT
MR SPROOD
MRS GRONGE

(The MANAGER is standing waiting. Enter MR SPROOD and MRS GRONGE, both looking anxious.)

MANAGER: Ah good morning Mrs Gronge, Mr Sprood. Do sit down.

MRS GRONGE: Er, there aren't any chairs.

MANAGER: What? Ah erm, *(calls off stage)* three chairs please.
(The ASSISTANT enters and faces the audience.)

ASSISTANT: *(Shouting)* Hip hip hooray, hip hip hooray, hip hip hooray!

MANAGER: *(Clips the ASSISTANT round the ear.)* No, you fool, we want three *chairs*.

ASSISTANT: Oooh sorry! *(Exits and returns carrying three chairs. The MANAGER, MRS GRONGE and MR SPROOD all sit. The ASSISTANT exits.)*

MANAGER: Now then, I'm sure you know why I've asked you to come and see me.

MR SPROOD: You were lonely?

MANAGER: No.

MRS GRONGE: We were lonely?

MANAGER: No. I've asked you to come and see me because you both owe me — I mean the shop — some money on your credit payments. *(There is a pause as MRS GRONGE and MR SPROOD look embarrassed.)*

MANAGER: Well?

MR SPROOD: Yes, I'm fine thanks.

MANAGER: *(Aside)* You could have fooled me. *(To them both)* Well, do you owe our shop some money?

BOTH: Yes.

MANAGER: And you realize that you've got behind with your credit payments?

BOTH: Yes.

MANAGER: So you've both got goods that you can't actually afford?

BOTH: Yes.

MANAGER: And so you have come here today...

BOTH: Yes.

MANAGER: To pay the rest of the money!

BOTH: No!

MANAGER: What?

MRS GRONGE: *(Falling on her knees)* Oh please, please, please forgive me, but I've got no money at all. But I should be getting some fairly soon...ish.

MR SPROOD: *(Falling on his knees)* Me too, sir. I would love to pay you. Really I would. I can't think of anything that would give me greater satisfaction. But I too am completely skint.

MANAGER: Oh come on. Get up both of you. *(They sit on the chairs.)* Let's have a look at what you have bought and see if we can sort something out. *(Calls off stage)* Files please. *(Enter the ASSISTANT with two nail files.)* Thank you ... what? No you fool, not files but *files*.

ASSISTANT: Oooh, sorry! *(Exits and returns with some papers. Hands them to the MANAGER.)*

MANAGER: Thank you. Now then Mr Sprood, I see you purchased the very latest Toshakai 500 watt infra-red remote control, midi-stacking Dolby quadraphonic Hi-Fi system, with integral compact disc player, three cassette decks, a short wave radio, two record decks, a graphic equalizer and built-in digital clock and telephone. The total retail value of this unit is £1,999.99. Mrs Gronge, you, on the other hand, bought an orange plastic hair brush worth £2.53. And neither of you has any money?

BOTH: No.

MANAGER: Ah, hmmm. Well it looks like there's only one thing I can do...

Forgiveness

TRAILER

Jesus put an ending on a story like this: he said, 'Forgive them both, because I have forgiven you.'

WORKSHOP

Have someone ready to ask the group what they would do if they were the shop manager. If you are feeling confident (or mad) get the group to write their endings and then act them out. You could award prizes for the best or funniest endings.

Read Jesus' story about the two men who were in debt (**Luke 7:41-42**) and get the group members to spot how the story ended. Both debtors were treated equally, even though their debts to the creditor were not the same by any means. Jesus was teaching Simon an essential lesson for all of us. None of us can pay God back for the debt of our sin. We owe him everything. We might not think we need forgiving as much as some other people, or we might feel as if we've let God down more than anyone else. Whoever we are, we all need to be forgiven, and none of us is unforgivable. If you own up to God that you need forgiveness because of your sin, he will cancel your debt and accept you as a forgiven member of his family.

DIRECTOR'S TIPS

☞ Make sure that when the performers sit on the chairs they can still be seen. This is particularly important for Mr Sprood and Mrs Gronge. Have their chairs set at an angle, and have the tallest person sitting upstage (furthest away from the audience) so that they don't hide the other person.

☞ Use this short sketch to start a good discussion.

☞ Make it corny by overplaying the shop assistant's jokes and hamming up Mrs Gronge and Mr Sprood's pleading.

Caiaphas's Catastrophic Caper

DELILAH and **BENJAMIN** — Two teenagers.
CAIAPHAS — A chief priest.

(*DELILAH is standing waiting. Enter BENJAMIN running.*)
BENJAMIN: Delilah, Delilah, Delilah, Delilah! (*He collides with DELILAH, knocking her over.*)
DELILAH: Benjamin! Why don't you watch where you're going?
BENJAMIN: Oh don't worry about that, I've got some great news.
DELILAH: Don't tell me, Bethlehem won last night.
BENJAMIN: No! More important than camel racing.
DELILAH: Well, I never thought I'd hear you say anything was more important than camel racing.
BENJAMIN: Will you just shut up and listen? I've seen him, he's alive!
DELILAH: Seen who?
BENJAMIN: Jesus! He's alive.
DELILAH: I don't believe you.
BENJAMIN: But why, why, why, Delilah?
DELILAH: Because, because, because, Benjamin, Jesus is dead, remember? He was killed last week.
BENJAMIN: I know that, but now he's alive.
DELILAH: Benjamin, how can he be alive? Is this some sort of joke? Because if it is, I don't think it's funny.
BENJAMIN: Of course it's not a joke. (*Enter CAIAPHAS who stands at a distance listening.*) Look, I was at a meeting with Peter and loads of Jesus' friends, when suddenly he was in the room with us. And it wasn't a ghost because he ate some fish. So there!
CAIAPHAS: Hello, young man. I couldn't help overhearing you just now. Did you say you'd seen Jesus?
BENJAMIN: Yes, I was in this room with.... (*DELILAH clasps her hand over BENJAMIN's mouth and pulls him away.*) What are you doing?
DELILAH: Do you know who that is? That is Caiaphas, one of the people who had Jesus killed. He works at the temple.
BENJAMIN: Are you sure?
DELILAH: Yes! Don't tell him anything.
CAIAPHAS: Well young man, have you seen Jesus? Have you? Have you?
BENJAMIN: Why do you want to know? So you can kill all his friends like you killed him? Only it didn't work because he's alive again.
CAIAPHAS: Ah, so you admit it, eh? I think it's time you came with me.
BENJAMIN: No, never.
(*There is a struggle. Caiaphas grabs BENJAMIN, who tries to run away. DELILAH also grabs Benjamin and they have a tug-of-war with him. Eventually CAIAPHAS wins and drags BENJAMIN off screaming.*)
DELILAH: (*Calling off*) Come back you thug! Leave him alone. (*To herself*) What am I going to do? Now they've got Benjamin they might do anything to him. I wonder if Jesus really is alive. Benjamin certainly thought so. But I must think of a way of rescuing Benjamin. (*She thinks for a moment.*) Ah, I have a cunning plan that will expose that cruel creep Caiaphas at his weakest point. I shall reduce him to a phobic frenzy and in the heat of a reptilian rampage we shall break Benjamin's bonds. But to make it work I shall need a super slippery slithery snake. (*She exits. Enter CAIAPHAS dragging BENJAMIN.*)
CAIAPHAS: Right! Now I've got you, I'm going to make you talk. (*He pushes BENJAMIN into a chair.*) And if you say Jesus is alive again I'll have to deal seriously with you. I might even sing to you.
BENJAMIN: Aaaarggh! No, not that!
(*Enter DELILAH carrying a rubber snake.*)
DELILAH: (*Aside*) OK Caiaphas. Your game's over. (*She throws a rubber snake at CAIAPHAS' neck and shouts*) Snake!
CAIAPHAS: Aaarggh! (*He grabs at the snake and has a violent struggle with it. In the course of his struggling he staggers off stage.*)
DELILAH: Are you all right?
BENJAMIN: Yeah. Thanks, Delilah, I thought I was done for there. Hey, we'd better go, or we're going to be late.
DELILAH: What for? Are we going to see Jesus?
BENJAMIN: I don't know, but unless we hurry we're going to miss the start of the camel race. (*He runs off.*)
DELILAH: (*To the audience*) Typical! (*She runs after him.*)

Resurrection

TRAILER

Did Jesus rise from the dead? Well, either he did or he didn't. What do you say?

WORKSHOP

Was Jesus really alive? Use the sketch as a discussion starter on the evidence for the Resurrection. Look at **John 20:24-31**. This is the incident which Benjamin reports to Delilah. Thomas, fairly understandably, had his doubts about what he had been told (i.e. that Jesus was alive). However, when Thomas saw Jesus he *knew* he was God.

After that Jesus said that those who had not seen, yet still believed would be blessed. Ask the group if they would have believed Benjamin, or would they have wanted proof like Thomas? *Compass Book 13* has a whole teaching session on the evidence for the Resurrection. See page 46 for details.

But does it matter that Jesus rose from the dead? Yes! Because all that Jesus claimed for himself depended on him coming back from the dead, and he did! So we know for sure that new life with God is a possibility for us.

DIRECTOR'S TIPS

☞ Make the most of the physical activity in the sketch. The tug of war needs to be very big and loud, and Caiaphas's fight with the snake should be completely over the top with plenty of screaming and struggling. The snake should win!

☞ Make Caiaphas a classic pantomime villain, or even the type of caped baddie who turned up in silent movies.

Playing Tonight

SANDRA and **TRACY** — Pop fans.
DEREK — Not a pop fan.

(*TRACY is listening to her personal stereo. She is wearing all the latest trendy gear, and I mean all. Enter SANDRA similarly dressed, very excited and carrying a copy of a teen-pop magazine. TRACY doesn't respond at all as she's too busy listening to her music.*)

SANDRA: 'Ere Trace, Trace have you seen this? Look there's a big article all about The Stunners. There's pictures of Steve Stunner, Simon Stunner, Stuart Stunner and the most dishy of them all...Bob. Not only that, but there's also a huge colour picture of them, look! (*Pause*) Tracy? Tracy? Are you listening to me? (*Shouts*) Tracy! (*Still no response, so SANDRA lifts one of the earphones and shouts*) Tracy!

TRACY: (*Turns off her stereo*) Oh hello Sandra, you been here long?

SANDRA: Yeah, ages. But look have you seen this article about The Stunners?

TRACY: The Stunners? Where? Show me, show me! Oh! Aren't they dreamy?

SANDRA: Yeah! Hey! Have you seen this month's edition of *Cool Music Monthly*? There's full-colour pictures of all the group in there.

TRACY: Really? Wow! I'd love to get a copy of that.

SANDRA: Yeah! Me too. (*They carry on reading their magazine. Enter DEREK carrying a magazine.*)

DEREK: Hi, Sandra! Hi, Tracy!

(*They both murmur hello from behind their magazine.*)

DEREK: Oh well, don't over-do the welcome will you?

TRACY: Oh what do you want, Derek? Can't you see we're busy reading about The Stunners?

DEREK: The Stunners? What are you reading about them for? They're awful.

SANDRA: Well we like them, so shove off!

TRACY: Yeah, go and read your *Train Spotters' Weekly* or whatever it is.

DEREK: What, this? (*He indicates his magazine.*) No, this is the latest edition of *Cool Music Monthly*.

(*He begins to walk off. SANDRA and TRACY go back to their magazine. They then stop, look at each other, look at Derek and scream very loudly. They drop their magazine, chase after Derek, push him over, snatch his magazine, run back and start reading it.*)

SANDRA: Oh look! There's a picture of Simon Stunner. What a hunk! (*They turn the page.*)

TRACY: Wow! And there's Stuart. What a dish! (*DEREK has got to his feet and is now standing between the girls, looking over their shoulders. They turn the page and scream loudly. DEREK reels backwards.*)

SANDRA: Oh wow! It's Bob, he's my fave.

DEREK: Will you two just grow up? Honestly! Look at you. You're like a couple of little children screaming and yelling.

TRACY: And why shouldn't we? You're just jealous because no one screams about you.

DEREK: But they're not even talented. They're useless.

SANDRA: No they're not. And we don't care what you think anyway.

TRACY: Hey! Look Sandra. It says here that The Stunners are going to be playing here in three weeks time. We've got to go!

SANDRA: Wow! Yeah! Come on. Let's go and get tickets before they sell out. (*The girls rush out taking DEREK'S magazine, but leaving their own.*)

DEREK: Oi! Come back with my magazine. Oh what's the use? I'll just have to read this, I suppose. (*He picks up their magazine and starts to flick through it.*) Hang on, what's this? Orifice and the Ear Benders are playing tonight! Oh wow! I've just got to see them, they're excellent! (*He runs off.*)

Worship

TRAILER

Who's really big enough to deserve your full, undivided love?

WORKSHOP

Read **2 Samuel 6:12-23**. This is the account of David bringing the Ark of God into Jerusalem. Get the group to visualise what the procession must have looked like. Bulls and calves were sacrificed after people had taken just six steps. David, the King, was dancing before the Lord with all his might and when they arrived in Jerusalem he handed out food to every person.

Throughout all this David's thoughts were on praising God, just like Sandra and Tracy were totally engrossed in The Stunners. Sandra and Tracy didn't worry about Derek's jibes because of their devotion to the group. In the same way David was not concerned when Michal started to criticize him, because he was dancing before God, not for the people around him.

Ask the group to think about the times when they are involved in worship. Where are we focusing our thoughts in those times? Are we able to concentrate on God's love? Or do other things fill our thoughts?

DIRECTOR'S TIPS

☞ Sandra and Tracy need to be completely unashamed in their devotion of The Stunners. Their costumes should be over the top, but it is important they don't feel self-conscious at the way they look.

☞ When Derek is pushed over, the impetus is on Derek to move in such a way that it appears as if he's been violently attacked. The more exaggerated Derek can make his fall the better.

It's a Fair Cop

MR MAL AREA — A Businessman.
RUTH — His Secretary.
WALLABY OF THE YARD — A Police Officer (male or female).

(Mr AREA is sitting working at his desk. There is a knock on the door and RUTH enters.)

RUTH: Mr Area, a police officer's here. He says he would like to see you immediately. *(She shows WALLABY in.)*

WALLABY: Right, thank you miss. I've seen him now. It's confirmed my worst suspicions. I'll be on my way.
(WALLABY leaves and after a moment of looking totally confused, MR AREA carries on with his work. There is a slight pause.)

WALLABY: *(Bursting back in)* Not so fast, sir! You are Mr Area — deny it if you dare!

MR AREA: I don't deny it.

WALLABY: Mr Mal Area?

MR AREA: I prefer to use my full name — Malcolm.

WALLABY: They told me over the radio you were a slippery character but you're not fast enough for Wallaby of the Yard!

MR AREA: I take it then that you, officer, are Wallaby of the Yard?

WALLABY: *(Proudly)* Yes sir, that's me, sir.

MR AREA: And would it, perchance, be too much to ask what all this bursting in and shouting at people is all about?

WALLABY: No sir, nothing is too much for Wallaby of the Yard! *(There is a slight pause.)*

MR AREA: Then what's it all about?

WALLABY: Ah yes, well you see sir, I just happen to be investigating the case of who painted Big Ben fluorescent yellow last night. A dastardly crime if ever there was one!

MR AREA: What?

WALLABY: Yes. We're looking for a criminal mind, and body I may add, of unparalleled ingenuity!

MR AREA: But ...

WALLABY: *(Leaning menacingly over the desk)* We 'appen to believe that it may well be the same person what made off with the Manchester Ship Canal last year.

MR AREA: Not the ...

WALLABY: Yes sir! *(Becoming quite excited)* We're on the trail of that landmark fiend, known throughout the underworld as *(dramatically)* Ben Nevis!

MR AREA: *(Almost pleading)* Officer, Officer!

WALLABY: What is it sir? Is there something you want to tell me, something you think I ought to know?

MR AREA: Officer, you can't possibly suspect me!?

WALLABY: *(Taken aback)* No sir, 'course not sir! I was just passing and noticed you'd parked your car on double yellow lines.

MR AREA: *(Stares at the officer for a second in disbelief and shock.)* What? You mean you burst in here — you take time off from a major investigation to, to tell me what I already know!

WALLABY: So you admit it then?

MR AREA: Of course I do, but, but ...

WALLABY: But it's still an offence, so I'm afraid I'm going to have to book you sir.

MR AREA: Oh, it's a fair cop!

WALLABY: Right then sir, let's be having you. You have the right to remain silent. You have the right to vast amounts of paint remover — oh no, that's not you, is it? Come along this way, let's be moving that vehicle. *(Exit)*

© CPAS 1994

Sin and Forgiveness

TRAILER

Which is more serious — parking on double yellow lines, or painting Big Ben yellow?
Which is more serious — stealing from a shop, or planting a bomb?
God hates any kind of wrong, so they're all pretty serious.

DIRECTOR'S TIPS

☞ Get plenty of humour in this sketch by making Wallaby a larger than life figure. Give him note books, a two-way radio and big boots. If you choose to give him a silly voice, make sure all the words can still be heard.

☞ Give people time to get the jokes and laugh. When people laugh, pause while the laughter dies down, otherwise they will miss the next part of the sketch and you will rob yourself of another well-earned laugh.

WORKSHOP

Many people think that only big sins count before God, and all the little things that we all do don't really matter. In the sketch Mal Area thought that Wallaby of the Yard was wasting his time on his illegally parked car while the landmark fiend Ben Nevis was still at large. As Wallaby pointed out, Mal Area had still committed an offence. The fact that it wasn't as serious as the other crimes didn't make it trivial.

Read **Psalm 51**. This is David asking for forgiveness for having committed adultery with Bathsheba and ordering the murder of her husband. In verse 5 David shows that he realizes that the problem runs deep. Sin has been a part of him since before he was born. Sin is not just what we do, but what we are. The sins we commit are a result of the way we are. Whoever we are, we need to come to God to ask his forgiveness as we promise to turn our backs on sin. Read on through verses 6 and 7 and note the confidence that David has about God's ability to forgive sin.

The Kept Promise

SALLY — in love with Steve but embarrassed to admit it.
STEVE — in love with Sally but embarrassed to admit it.
TRACY — Tim's girlfriend.
TIM — Tracy's boyfriend.

(*SALLY is wandering around looking bored and fed up. She is carrying a music cassette. STEVE enters.*)

STEVE: Hi Sally, something up?

SALLY: Sun, sky, seagulls.

STEVE: Ho, ho what scintillating sarcasm, but why so sad Sally? Shouldn't you be celebrating your sixteenth soon?

SALLY: Sure, it's my sixteenth today, but my silly sister sent me The Stunners' latest tape *Sixteen Sloppy Songs Sung Slowly*.

STEVE: Sharon sent you The Stunners?

SALLY: Sure, but I'm short of a stereo.

STEVE: (*Becoming dramatically romantic*) Sally, since you stole my soul, I shall soon supply you with a splendid stereo, so you can successfully sound out The Stunners' *Sixteen Sloppy Songs Sung Slowly*.

SALLY: Stop saying stupid sentences.

STEVE: Stop here in suspense and see: soon a superior stereo shall be supplied. (*He exits and TIM and TRACY enter from the other direction.*)

TRACY: Sally, triumphant tidings to you today!

SALLY: (*Jumps when she hears TRACY*) 'Strewth Tracy, you shocked me, sneaking up so silently.

TRACY: Terribly tactless I know, but why this timid temperament?

SALLY: Steve's said he's shopping for a stereo so that I can sound out The Stunners' *Sixteen Sloppy Songs Sung Slowly*, which Sharon sent for my sixteenth.

TIM: Twaddle! Steve's too tight to buy tape recorders.

TRACY: Tragically, Tim's totally true. Steve, though tanned, tall and terrific, is a trying troublemaker.

SALLY: Stop speaking such slander. Steve sincerely said he shall soon surprise us with a smashing stereo.

TIM: Trust Tracy, Steve's a typicaly turbulent toad. His tedious trickery can be terribly traumatic.

SALLY: Cease smearing Steve's soft and soppy sentiments. Steve's solution is sincere. (*Enter STEVE with a present for SALLY. She opens it. It's a personal stereo.*)

STEVE: Hello Tim, Tracy. Come to celebrate Sally's sixteenth? I've surprised her with a splendid stereo.

SALLY: Oh Steve, you are simply stunning. (*They walk off as romantically as you can get away with.*)

TRACY: (*To TIM*) Too tight eh? A typical turbulent toad? You total twit! (*She storms off with TIM following.*)

God's Promises

TRAILER

We make promises and try to keep them. God makes promises and always keeps them.

WORKSHOP

Ask the group members what was the last promise they made. Did they keep it?

In the sketch both Tracy and Tim thought that Steve would break his promise. Despite their arguments and objections Sally continued to believe in Steve and was finally rewarded with a stereo. Steve kept his promise. God has made many promises to his people, but they aren't all carried out when we think they ought to be.

Read **Matthew 12:15-21**. Although this passage was originally written many hundreds of years before Jesus was born, he used it to show that he was the one God had promised to send. Throughout his gospel, Matthew is at pains to show that Jesus was a promise that God was keeping to his people. You could look through Matthew's gospel to find some of the other prophesies (or promises) that Matthew pointed out had been fulfilled by the coming of Jesus. Matthew's gospel was aimed at the Jews to whom God had been promising a Messiah for hundreds of years. Jesus was God's way of keeping his promise.

DIRECTOR'S TIPS

☞ The use of alliterations means that the style of the sketch is very strong, and it can be easy for the message to get lost. Make sure the sketch is very visual, with easily seen props and big gestures and facial expressions so that everyone is clear about the plot.

☞ Not only do the lines need to be learned well, they also need to be delivered clearly. This means the sketch will probably seem slow to the performers. But if the performers come in crisply 'on cue', the sketch won't seem slow to the audience. See Top Tip number 2 on page 4 for hints on how to do this.

☞ Make sure that the performers have plenty of time to learn their lines and rehearse this sketch. It's one of the few in the book that hasn't got any room for improvisation and witty ad libs (unless, of course, you can keep the alliterations going).

What Would You Do?

PERCY CUTION — A thug.
HARRY SMENT — A thug.
VIC TIMM — A Christian.
PASSER-BY

---

[1] *(VIC is carrying some very heavy shopping. Enter HARRY and PERCY.)*
PERCY: Oi Harry, isn't that Vic Thingy?
HARRY: What, Vic Timm? Yeah, I think it is. *(Calls out)* Oi Vic! What are you up to, you great jessy?
VIC: *(Pleasantly)* Oh, hi Harry.
HARRY: Harry Sment to you.
VIC: Er yeah, Harry Sment. Who's this?
HARRY: This is my mate Percy Cution, and he thinks you're a right nerd.
PERCY: Yeah, what've you got in your shopping bag — a present for mummy? *(They push him around and look in the bags.)*
VIC: No, get off will yer. It's some food for Mr Phillips. He can't get out of his house.
HARRY: Aaaah! Doing our good deed for the day, are we? Being a good creepy Christian are we?
PERCY: I hate Christians. I always want to hit them *(They get a bit rougher.)*
VIC: Will you get off?
HARRY: Oh go on. Clear off, you pathetic creep, and don't come round here again with your stupid shopping.
VIC: I'm going shopping for Mr Phillips whether you like it or not. *(They exit.)*

[2] *(VIC is carrying some very heavy shopping. Enter HARRY and PERCY.)*
HARRY: I don't believe it, that pratt Vic is doing some more shopping.
PERCY: Let's go and sort him out. Oi Vicky, what are you doing round here?
VIC: Oh just some more shopping, Mr Phillips still can't get out you know.
HARRY: We don't care about Mr Phillips, we just don't want to see you around here again. *(They push him around and call him names. VIC hangs on to the shopping and doesn't retaliate.)*
PERCY: Oi Harry, this weed's not even brave enough to fight back. Let's not waste our time on him. *(VIC exits almost cheerfully.)*
HARRY: He's a bit odd, that Vic.
PERCY: You're telling me! Doing all that shopping and stuff.
HARRY: No, not that. I mean he didn't fight back. He almost seemed happy, 'cos he's a Christian yer know. Probably his God makes him like getting beat up.
PERCY: *(Very confused)* Yeah, probably Harry. *(They exit.)*

[3] *(VIC is carrying some very heavy shopping. Enter HARRY and PERCY.)*
PERCY: Would you believe it, Harry? That wally is back again. I've had enough. Let's sort him out.
HARRY: Good idea. Oi Vic, we've told you not to come round here again.
VIC: Yeah, well I've still got some shopping to do for Mr Phillips.
PERCY: We don't care, but we're going to sort you out. *(They start to beat up VIC. He doesn't retaliate and hangs on to his shopping. Enter a PASSER-BY, running.)*
PASSER-BY: Hey you two, get off him.
HARRY: Flippin' 'eck Percy let's get out of here. *(They run off.)*
VIC: Thanks pal.
PASSER-BY: Come on, if we're quick we can catch them and teach them a proper lesson.
VIC: No, I don't want to; it'll do no good.
PASSER-BY: Don't be stupid, they're not that tough.
VIC: Oh I know that, but they need someone to forgive them.
PASSER-BY: What? Don't talk wet.
VIC: No, straight up — they need someone to forgive them. *(VIC exits. The PASSER-BY is very confused and exits.)*

[4] *(VIC is carrying some very heavy shopping. Enter HARRY and PERCY.)*
PERCY: *(Very angry)* I do not believe it! That dingo brain is back again. Well I've had enough, he's getting it now.
HARRY: Come on then, let's get rid of him for good.
PERCY: Oi you!
VIC: Oh hello. Nice weather for the time of year.
HARRY: Shut up! We've told you not to come round here before, so don't say we didn't warn you. *(They beat him up viciously and throw his shopping around. PERCY suddenly produces a weapon — knife/bike chain etc.)*
PERCY: Now listen scum, we've been gentle with you till now. But if you ever come round here again you'll be feeling this. *(They exit.)*
VIC: *(To audience)* Well blow this for a laugh. Next week I'm using different shops! *(Exit)*

Persecution

TRAILER

Being a Christian is going to mean suffering. But it is God who shows us how to get through.

WORKSHOP

Each of the four scenes highlights a different reaction to suffering. After the sketch has been performed look at the following passages to show how these principles are there for us to learn from in the Bible.

a. Acts 5:17-21 — They carried on despite the danger of death.

b. Acts 5:41 — They were joyful and felt privileged.

c. Acts 7:57-60 — They forgave those causing their suffering.

d. Acts 8:1 — When things were impossible, they witnessed elsewhere.

Use the sketch and these Bible passages to lead into a discussion on how we suffer today because we are Christians. Think of some practical ways we can support one another and grow in our faith through persecution.

DIRECTOR'S TIPS

☞ When Vic is beaten up in the final scene, make sure the person playing him doesn't get hurt. The way to do this is for Vic's *reactions* to show that he's been hit. If Harry throws a punch (which will miss Vic) Vic should scream in pain and throw himself as if he has been hit. With practice this can look very effective.

☞ Percy Cution and Harry Sment should get more aggressive with each scene. They want to be nasty, rather than comic, bad guys by the final scene.

☞ Either perform all four scenes one after another, or perform them at different slots throughout your programme.

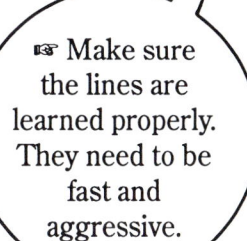

☞ Make sure the lines are learned properly. They need to be fast and aggressive.

Lord Wormington Squirrel and his Faithful Butler, Boote

LORD WORMINGTON SQUIRREL — A pompous aristocrat.

BOOTE — His aged, faithful and almost completely useless butler.

(*LORD WORMINGTON SQUIRREL is sitting in lordly state reading a paper.*)

LORD: (*Calling*) Boote! Boote! Where are you, man?

BOOTE: (*Hobbling in*) Here, m'Lord. Here I am.

LORD: Come on man! Get a move on! Want some tea Boote!

BOOTE: Thank you very kindly, sir. Don't mind if I do. Very nice of you to offer, sir.

LORD: Not you, you fool! Me! I want some tea. Get some.

BOOTE: Oh yes, quite sir. Right away, m'Lord. Quick as a flash, sir. Here in a jiffy, your Lordship. (*He exits bowing. LORD WORMINGTON resumes reading his paper. After a short interval BOOTE returns carrying a hammer.*)

BOOTE: Here we are, sir.

LORD: What's that?

BOOTE: (*Looks at the hammer with a slightly puzzled expression as if he doesn't know where it came from.*) A hammer, sir. Yes, definitely a hammer.

LORD: What's if for, Boote?

BOOTE: (*Thinks for a moment*) Hitting things, sir. Nails or beetles. Very useful for squashing school peas too, m'Lord.

LORD: I don't mean that, you fool! I mean why have you brought it to me? I want some tea!

BOOTE: Ah yes, sir. Good point, sir. Not very useful for that, sir. No definitely no good under those circumstances at all, m'Lord. No indeed.

LORD: Blast! No time for tea now. I've got to see my accountant. Get the Rolls, Boote.

BOOTE: Right, m'lord. Straight away, m'Lord. You leave it to me, sir. Yes indeed, your Lordship. Quick as a flash. Roll out the Rolls...ha, ha, ha, ha.

LORD: Oh get on with it, man. (*BOOTE exits and soon returns with a tin opener.*) Got the Rolls, Boote?

BOOTE: (*Looking surprised*) No, sir.

LORD: What! What have you got, Boote?

BOOTE: This! (*He holds up the tin opener with great pride.*)

LORD: (*Almost in tears*) Why? Why Boote? Why?

BOOTE: (*Enjoying the opportunity to teach on his favourite subject*) Well, you put this part on the top of the tin, you see, and then carefully turn this handle here and hey presto! it opens the tin. Very cunning, m'Lord. Fastest thig for opening tins I know — excepting my Aunt Agatha's front teeth, sir. Now there's a pair of gnashers, m'Lord...

LORD: (*Desperately trying to control himself*) Boote! Why don't you ever do as I ask? I only want you to do as I ask. It's not too much to hope for is it? Just to do what I ask.

BOOTE: (*Looks very surprised*) Do what you say, m'Lord? Goodness gracious me! What a thought! I never realized you wanted me to do what you said... (*BOOTE exits, shaking his head and looking surprised. LORD WORMINGTON exits, crying.*)

Obedience

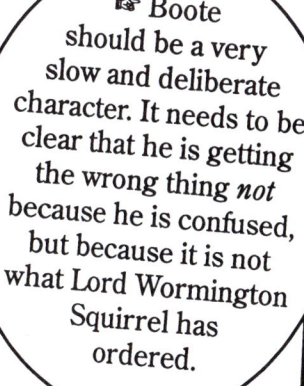

TRAILER

Jesus said, 'If you love me, do what I tell you'. Do you?

WORKSHOP

Ask the group members if they like being told what to do. Are there some people or commands we obey more readily than others?

Read **Matthew 7:24-27**. The parable of the wise and foolish builders comes at the end of Jesus' Sermon on the Mount. The point Jesus was making was that people needed not only to hear his words, but to put them into practice as well. If we hear what Jesus is saying and then ignore it, we are as useless as Boote. He might be quite a nice character, but as a butler he is a failure. The point of being a butler is to obey. Jesus wants us to obey him because he knows what is best for us.

DIRECTOR'S TIPS

☞ Lord Wormington should not laugh or even smile at Boote's antics. This will need practice. It requires great concentration to avoid laughing in a sketch, but it's worth the effort.

☞ Boote should be a very slow and deliberate character. It needs to be clear that he is getting the wrong thing *not* because he is confused, but because it is not what Lord Wormington Squirrel has ordered.

☞ Lord Wormington Squirrel should remain pompous throughout the sketch.

Empty-handed

MR HATTON — A passenger for flight REV 320.
STACEY — Check-in receptionist.
MRS SEYMORE — Another passenger.
AIRLINE WORKERS

(STACEY is sitting at the check-in desk. MR HATTON enters loaded down with as many suitcases, rucksacks and bags as possible. He also has a small carrier bag that is hidden from view.)

MR HATTON: Good morning. Is this the check-in point for flight REV 320?

STACEY: That's right sir. Do you have your ticket?

MR HATTON: *(He puts down his luggage and begins to hunt for the ticket.)* Ha ha yes, I know it's here somewhere...now let me think, I had it when I left home this morning. It's always happening to me, this sort of thing. *(Suddenly finds it)* Ah here it is. There you are.

STACEY: Thank you, Mr *(reads the ticket)* Hatton. Yes, everything appears to be in order. Please proceed to Gate 3 and your plane will leave in thirty minutes.

MR HATTON: Erm, haven't you forgotten something?

STACEY: I don't think so, sir, why?

MR HATTON: What about my luggage?

STACEY: What luggage would that be, sir?

MR HATTON: Are you all right, Miss?

STACEY: I think so. Why, what appears to be the problem, Mr Hatton?

MR HATTON: *(Looks at the luggage and then at STACEY in disbelief.)* Well Stacey, I don't know if you've noticed, but I'm surrounded by all this luggage, and I would like to take it on the plane with me. *(STACEY bursts into laughter)* I'm sorry, did I say something funny?

STACEY: No, excuse me, it's just I thought you said you wanted to take all that luggage on the plane.

MR HATTON: I did, and I do.

STACEY: Well, I'm sorry but there's no luggage allowed on the plane.

MR HATTON: Pardon?

STACEY: The ticket clearly says, if you would care to look, that there is no luggage allowed as all needs will be met at the destination.

MR HATTON: Well, that's as maybe, but I've spent my life's savings on some very nice going-away things, and I would like to take them with me.

STACEY: Well, I'm sorry but that is out of the question.

(Enter MRS SEYMORE with no luggage and in a rush)

MRS SEYMORE: Is this the place for flight REV 320?

STACEY: That's right. Do you have a ticket?

MR HATTON: Er excuse me, but I'm being served here.

MRS SEYMORE: Oh sorry, I didn't think you would be on this flight with all that luggage.

STACEY: *(Handing back MRS SEYMORE'S ticket)* Yes, this gentleman seems to want to take his luggage with him. However, your ticket is in order so if you would like to proceed to Gate 3, the plane will be leaving in about twenty five minutes.

MRS SEYMORE: *(To MR HATTON)* Are you really trying to take all that stuff with you? What a scream! *(She exits laughing to herself about MR HATTON.)*

MR HATTON: OK. Look, I'll do a deal with you. I'll get rid of the stuff I don't need and only take the bare essentials. *(He looks through all the luggage and eventually brings out the small carrier that was hidden from view.)* There, you can keep that bag and I'll just take this little lot.

STACEY: The answer is still no. You can't take anything with you. You're just going to have to leave it all behind.

MR HATTON: No, no I'm not going to. I can't survive without all my things. I've worked hard to get all these things and I'm not leaving them now. *(He starts to clutch his belongings.)*

STACEY: I'm sorry, Mr Hatton, but you can't take those things with you and now it's time for you to board the plane.

MR HATTON: Well, I'm not going to. I shall stay here with my things for ever.

STACEY: That also is impossible, Mr Hatton.

(From now all action is silent. A group of AIRLINE WORKERS enters. They relieve MR HATTON of his luggage. MR HATTON struggles to hold on, but eventually fails. The AIRLINE WORKERS lift MR HATTON onto their shoulders, so that he is lying face up as if in a coffin. They carry him off slowly. MR HATTON is completely motionless. STACEY puts a 'closed' sign on the desk and walks off slowly behind the AIRLINE WORKERS. The luggage is left behind.)

© CPAS 1994

Death

TRAILER

There isn't one. The sketch speaks for itself really. The best thing would be thirty seconds silence to let people think about what they have just seen.

WORKSHOP

Read the parable of the rich fool (**Luke 12:15-21**). Mr Hatton, along with countless other people all over the world, had lived his life like the man in the parable. They had tried to be as rich as possible. What Mr Hatton had to learn, though, was that his possessions didn't count for anything in the end. He couldn't take them with him, nor could he stay behind to keep them. The man in the parable had to learn the same lesson, he also had to learn that it is God who decides when we die; we can't decide that for ourselves.

Both these characters needed to learn that trying to get as much money, possessions and status as possible is ultimately pointless. It is our relationship to God that is the most important thing.

DIRECTOR'S TIPS

☞ The end of the sketch should be a complete contrast to the rest. The action should be slightly slower than normal, and should be exaggerated a bit. If you can alter the lighting for this part (or light it with a strobe) it would help to enhance the dramatic effect and show that the sketch is actually not about an airline at all, but about death.

☞ Make sure Mr Hatton is loaded down to a ridiculous degree. The more bags and cases the funnier and the better.

☞ All the performers need to concentrate on not laughing as that will destroy the atmosphere.

☞ Stuff the bags with paper to make them look as if they are full.

☞ Mr Hatton will need to act as if the bags are heavy with lots of grimacing and grunting.

☞ Make sure that the small carrier is completely hidden until it is needed.

☞ Practise lifting Mr Hatton up, so that it can be done smoothly and with minimum effort.

Innocent

MR CORPUSTY — Headmaster at St Colditz boarding school.
GLOSSOP — A pupil at St Colditz boarding school.
BELPER — A pupil at St Colditz boarding school.
CRUDWELL — A pupil at St Colditz boarding school.

---

[1] *(MR CORPUSTY is siting at a desk.)*
MR CORPUSTY: *(Shouting)* Belper, I will see you now.
(Enter BELPER)
MR CORPUSTY: Now then, Belper, I'm sure you know why I've asked you to come here.
BELPER: No, sir.
MR CORPUSTY: What do you mean 'no'? I should have thought that even to someone of your limited intelligence it would be obvious why you've had to come and see me again.
BELPER: No, I'm afraid not, Mr Corpusty, sir
MR CORPUSTY: I see, and does it give you a clue if I say *cabbage*?
BELPER: I'm sorry sir?
MR CORPUSTY: Cabbage, boy, cabbage. You left some of your cabbage at lunch time today.
BELPER: But I didn't have any cabbage
MR CORPUSTY: That's got nothing to do with it boy. Not eating your cabbage is a serious offence here at St Colditz School. You will therefore receive the full punishment. Six of the best. *(He reaches for his cane.)*
BELPER: But that's not fair. I have sandwiches. *(They freeze as BELPER is looking worried and MR CORPUSTY is flexing his cane and looking malicious.)*

[2] *(MR CORPUSTY is sitting at a desk.)*
MR CORPUSTY: *(Shouting)* Crudwell, I will see you now.
(Enter CRUDWELL)
MR CORPUSTY: Now then, Crudwell, I'm sure you know why I've asked you to come here.
CRUDWELL: No, sir.
MR CORPUSTY: What do you mean 'no'? I should have thought that even to someone of your limited intelligence it would be obvious why you've had to come and see me again.
CRUDWELL: No I'm afraid not, Mr Corpusty, sir.
MR CORPUSTY: I see, and does it give you a clue if I say *turnip*?
BELPER: I'm sorry sir?
MR CORPUSTY: Turnip, boy, turnip. Yesterday you attacked the school eel collection with a turnip.
CRUDWELL: That wasn't me, sir. It was Trantlebeg.
MR CORPUSTY: Trantlebeg? How dare you slander that fine boy?
CRUDWELL: But everyone saw him do it.
MR CORPUSTY: Well, he very sensibly came and told me that you had done it and that he had tried to save the eels.
CRUDWELL: Save them? He ate them!
MR CORPUSTY: Aaah, what a sacrifice that boy made. Well, here at St Colditz School we take attacking eels with a turnip very seriously. So you will get the punishment. Six of the best.
CRUDWELL: But it can't have been me. I wasn't here yesterday.*(They freeze as CRUDWELL is looking worried and MR CORPUSTY is flexing his cane and looking malicious.)*

[3] *(MR CORPUSTY is sitting at a desk.)*
MR CORPUSTY: *(Shouting)* Glossop, I will see you now.
(Enter GLOSSOP)
MR CORPUSTY: Now then, Glossop, I'm sure you know why I've asked you to come here.
GLOSSOP: No, sir.
MR CORPUSTY: What do you mean 'no'? I should have thought that even to someone of your limited intelligence it would be obvious why you've had to come and see me again.
GLOSSOP: No, I'm afraid not, Mr Corpusty, sir.
MR CORPUSTY: I see, and does it give you a clue if I say *cup cake*?
GLOSSOP: I'm sorry sir?
MR CORPUSTY: Cup cake, boy, cup cake. You force-fed the school stick insect twenty three cup cakes *(pause)*. Well, don't you have anything to say for yourself? *(Pause)* What, nothing at all? *(Pause)* Aren't you going to scream and fight like the others? Because I know you didn't do it. Trantlebeg came and told me, but he always lies. Still not going to say anything? Right. Well, I'd better just punish you and get it over with.*(They freeze with GLOSSOP looking calm and MR CORPUSTY flexing his cane and looking confused.)*

How did Jesus respond to suffering?

TRAILER

Is there anything worse than doing nothing wrong and being killed for it? That is what happened to Jesus.

WORKSHOP

Ask the group to identify the differences and similarities between the scenes. Look at **Luke 23:13-25**. Both Pilate and Herod failed to find any reason for condemning Jesus. In fact their agreement brought them closer together because until then they had been enemies. Had Jesus protested his innocence or stuck up for himself at all, he almost certainly would have been released. Instead, just like Glossop, he allowed himself to suffer. But Jesus allowed himself to suffer and die because he knew there was no other way to achieve what God wanted. Look back to **Luke 22:42**.

DIRECTOR'S TIPS

☞ Belper and Corpusty should look absolutely terrified when facing punishment. The best way to do this is with good facial expressions, so make sure the performers are facing the audience.

☞ Crudwell should work hard at crisp pronunciation so that the names and the crimes are as clear as possible. An over-the-top pompous voice is a good idea, so that the humour of the unusual names and punishments is exploited to its full extent.

☞ The three scenes of this sketch can either be performed straight after each other, or during an evening's programme.

☞ Make Crudwell really vindictive and malicious when dealing out the punishment.

Beyond the Game

DRANBO THE DESTROYER — A character in a computer game.

ZYPONG THE ZURGLE — A character in a computer game.

(DRANBO is looking around taking the occasional potshot at flying Scrimbags. ZYPONG enters having escaped from Quijop the Zurgle Eater.)

DRANBO: Hey, it's Zypong the Zurgle! What are you up to?

ZYPONG: (*Sounding bored*) Oh, hi, Dranbo the Destroyer. I'm just waiting to go up to Level 8 to conquer Flipslap the Fearsome Flapper.

DRANBO: Level 8? Wowzy! Your score must be hugely high!

ZYPONG: Yep, I'm on 220,000 — a new record, I think. But who cares?

DRANBO: Hey, look out. Here comes a Belchicrud! (*They both jump out of the way.*) Phew! That was just too close for my liking. I've only got two lives left. Have you really got 220,000? That's just ace! How can you stand there and say 'Who cares?'

ZYPONG: Yeah, but what's it all for? I mean, we do all this dodging Belchidruds, and you shoot Scrimbags and no one even knows we're here.

DRANBO: Well, Ian knows when he's playing the game.

ZYPONG: Ian? Oh he really cares, doesn't he? I suppose that's why he puts us in his school bag next to his peanut butter, marmalade and tomato sauce sandwiches. And if he cares so much, how come he drops dirty socks on us in his bedroom, eh? You know, sometimes I wish the person playing him would just leave him lying around.

DRANBO: (*Shouting*) Belchicrud! (*They both jump.*) But, Zypong, Ian doesn't have anyone playing him.

ZYPONG: Doesn't have anyone? What are you talking about? He must have someone. Everyone is being played by someone.

DRANBO: Not Ian. He lives outside the game.

ZYPONG: How can he live outside the game, Dranbo? Who would keep his score?

DRANBO: But he doesn't have a score!

ZYPONG: He must have a score. You get one at the start of the game.

DRANBO: But Ian was around before the start of the game.

ZYPONG: Now you're talking rubbish.

DRANBO: No! He was around before the start of the game, he lives outside of this game and he doesn't have a score!

ZYPONG: Huh! Next you're going to tell me that he's not even afraid of Flipslap the Fearsome Flapper.

DRANBO: No, he's not.

ZYPONG: Look pal, you're off your head. You should get help. Try Diamootinck the Demon Doctor on Level 5, he's very good.

DRANBO: But wait...

ZYPONG: See yer, I'm off to Level 8. There's Belchicruds to sort out, you know.

(ZYPONG flies off. DRANBO looks fed up and then takes his frustration out on a flying Scrimbag. He storms off moodily.)

The Nature of God

TRAILER

God said, 'My thoughts are not your thoughts, neither are your ways my ways.' (**Isaiah 55:8**) Isn't it good to know there is someone bigger than all of us?

DIRECTOR'S TIPS

☞ The sketch is set inside an imaginary computer game, so this is your big chance to dress up as space warriors and leap around!

☞ Dranbo should spend time at the beginning shooting the imaginary Scrimbags.

☞ Practise the names of the characters carefully, so that the performers don't trip over them.

☞ You could give Dranbo a water pistol as a gun. He can pretend to use it through the whole sketch, but not actually squirt it. Then at the very end he can pretend to shoot a Scrimbag that is above the audience, and soak the people at the front!

☞ If you are wondering what all the Belchicruds, Scrimbags and Zurgles are supposed to look like, don't ask me. I just made the names up!

WORKSHOP

Ask the group how they would describe God to their friends. In the sketch Zypong assumes Ian must be living inside a game, with a score. He is unable to comprehend any other way of existing. When we try to understand God we often have the same problem as Zypong. Everyone we know is born, gets old and dies, so it's very difficult to envisage a God who does none of those things. Even Jesus, who did do these things, was living in heaven before he came to earth and is living there now. Read **Exodus 3:13,14**. Here Moses is asking God who he is. The answer God gives shows us what he is like. When God said, 'I AM WHO I AM', the meaning was, 'I AM WHO I AM, AND I WILL BE WHO I WILL BE.' In other words God is always there and is always the same.

In **Isaiah 55: 8,9** we read that God's ways and thoughts are beyond any of ours. We must remember that God is not just a powerful person, he is God. Therefore, there will always be things that we don't know about God.

Be Prepared

BOB — Dressed for Summer (shorts, T shirt and shades), but not stupidly.
NORMAN — Carries an open umbrella.
THE MAN — Dressed similarly to Bob.
THE PHANTOM WATER THROWER — Throwing water!

(BOB enters dressed for Summer, but not stupidly. NORMAN enters carrying an open umbrella.)

NORMAN: Hey, Bob! What are you dressed like that for? Shouldn't you be getting ready for the water?

BOB: I am. I followed the instructions instead of just getting an umbrella.

NORMAN: Oh, you don't still listen to that rubbish, do you? I sort things out for myself, that's why I brought an umbrella.

BOB: Oh yeah?

NORMAN: Yeah. And anyway, who wants to go round looking like a jerk all their lives? *(BOB looks at NORMAN'S umbrella.)* Hey look, you might think an umbrella is stupid, but everyone has got one. We've got ourselves prepared and you ought to do the same.

BOB: I've told you, I am. I'm dressed like this because *he* is.

NORMAN: He is, he is...! How do you know, eh? And how do you know it's a he? It could be a she or an it for all we know.

BOB: Look, I've got a note from him here. *(He produces a piece of paper from his pocket.)* It tells us exactly how to prepare ourselves for the water and why we should bother.

NORMAN: You've got a note! You don't half talk a load of rubbish sometimes.

BOB: Well, that's what you think. But you want to look out because it's nearly time.

NORMAN: *(Sounding a bit worried)* Is it? Well, I'm ready.

(They both wait. BOB looks relaxed. NORMAN gradually starts looking worried. Eventually we hear the sound of someone approaching. THE MAN enters from the right carrying a parcel. He looks very intently at NORMAN looking hard at the umbrella. NORMAN tries in vain to hide it. THE MAN looks at BOB.)

THE MAN: *(To BOB)* Here, take this and come with me.

(He gives BOB a parcel. BOB opens it and brings out a personal stereo. He looks very pleased with it, puts it on and follows THE MAN off to the right, grooving. NORMAN watches them go and looks nervously at the audience. As he does this THE PHANTOM WATER THROWER enters from the left and throws water at Norman and soaks him. NORMAN gives an anguished scream and exits left.)

Holy Living

TRAILER

Christians live the way God tells them to. They find out what God says in the Bible.

WORKSHOP

In the sketch Bob was an example of what it means to live in a way that pleases God. Read through **1 Peter 1:13-25 to 1 Peter 2:12**. The reading could be split up into small, manageable sections. Give each section to a pair or small group to look at. Give them a few minutes to read their section and then invite them to tell the rest of the group what they have learned. This will enable the group to get to grips with the whole passage, without having to read vast amounts.

In his letters Peter was telling the churches about what Christians have to look forward to, the hope that we have. In this passage he is stressing the importance of living in a way that pleases God now. When we do that we will be truly prepared for when Jesus comes back, and won't be taken by surprise. We try to live a holy life because we know that God is holy.

DIRECTOR'S TIPS

☞ If you are performing this sketch in a group session, have the next item prepared and ready to start immediately the sketch has finished. Water being thrown always gets people excited. The best way to use this excitement is to go straight into an activity. Trying to have a quiet reflective time of prayer straight after this sketch is almost certainly doomed to failure!

☞ Keep the ending a secret from the group, otherwise they will be waiting for the water and will ignore the rest of the sketch.

☞ The amount of water thrown by the Phantom Water Thrower will depend on the type of room you're in and whether Norman can swim! You can use anything from a water pistol to a water cannon.

☞ Throw the water straight at Norman, so he is soaked and the umbrella is shown to be useless.

All Change

ZACCHAEUS — The tax collector.
MR WATT — A tax payer.

(*ZACCHAEUS is sitting at his desk. Enter Mr WATT.*)

ZACCHAEUS: Roll up, roll up. Come and pay your taxes. Taxes, lovely taxes! Step this way for tax payment.
WATT: There you go, Zacchaeus. (*He puts some money on the table.*)
ZACCHAEUS: Name?
WATT: Watt.
ZACCHAEUS: What's your name?
WATT: Yes it is.
ZACCHAEUS: Yes it is what?
WATT: Watt's my name.
ZACCHAEUS: Don't you know?
WATT: Don't I know what?
ZACCHAEUS: What is your name?
WATT: Watt is my name!
ZACCHAEUS: (*He thinks for a while.*) Oh I see, your name is Watt.
WATT: Correct.
ZACCHAEUS: Oh good, because you owe me £50.
WATT: How much?
ZACCHAEUS: £60.
WATT: Hang on, you just said £50. You've changed it.
ZACCHAEUS: No I haven't. It's been £70 all along.
WATT: It keeps going up! Will you stop altering the amount!
ZACCHAEUS: I haven't altered it. I'm merely taking into account current fluctuation levels, stock market trends and my holiday.
WATT: I'm not paying for your holiday!
ZACCHAEUS: Ah well, you don't have to. You see we've developed an entirely new form of tax for people like you. If you pay £80 per annum then thirty per cent goes to the standard tax, twenty five per cent goes to a new index-linked tax which means that all the money goes straight to Caesar without stopping to benefit any of the poor on the way. The final forty per cent goes to a brand new Empire Expansion Tax: this enables us to take over more of the world for a greater profit margin, thereby easing the financial burden on our own constituents who are then in a position to pay more to the Caesar's Christmas Party Benefit Tax. You, therefore, can rest assured that all your money goes straight to the areas where it's needed most. See?
WATT: (*Very confused*) Eeeeer, well not really, 'cos isn't that tax more expensive?
ZACCHAEUS: Well, there are certain financial restrictions that we have to impose to cover the administrative costs. However, were you to start paying this tax now, by the time you are (*does a quick calculation*) 128 you won't have to pay any more tax at all. This is due to the new tax ceiling imposed by the Chancellor at the last budget during his fiscal policy review. Is that clear enough?
WATT: Well, er, yeah, I suppose so.
ZACCHAEUS: Great! Now that'll be £90 plus commission — £154, thank you. (*WATT puts a lot more money on the table which ZACCHAEUS snatches up greedily.*) Ooooh look at the time! I must dash! That Jesus is due to come by soon. I must see him. I've heard he can do some pretty amazing things. (*He exits.*)
WATT: Yeah, well I doubt if he'll be able to understand you. No one is that clever. £154 — how can taxes be that expensive? (*He starts to walk off, moaning. Enter ZACCHAEUS very excited.*)
ZACCHAEUS: Watt, Watt, don't go! Boy, have I got a treat for you!
WATT: I doubt it.
ZACCHAEUS: What? No don't start. But look, I've changed.
WATT: Rubbish, you were wearing those clothes when you left.
ZACCHAEUS: Eh? No look, I've changed. I want to give you back all the money I've cheated you out of.
WATT: You what?
ZACCHAEUS: No, you Watt. Me Zacchaeus — ha ha ha! Anyway, look I've got your money. You should have paid £50 but in the end I took £154. So I'm giving back £104 plus an extra £320 for clerical errors that I've made in the past.
WATT: You're trying to give me money! No way! There has got to be something dodgy about this. You never give money to anybody.
ZACCHAEUS: I didn't used to, but I've changed. Look, just take it will you 'cos I'm in a bit of a rush. I've got several other people to pay back. (*ZACCHAEUS gives away the money eagerly.*)
WATT: Weird! That guy is cuckoo! He'll probably be back soon demanding it all back... unless of course I've spent it all by then. (*He exits eagerly.*)

Zacchaeus

TRAILER

Jesus changes people. You may think Christian behaviour is weird. But what's your definition of normal?

WORKSHOP

Look at **Luke 19:1-10**. Note down the reaction of Zacchaeus to Jesus. Then get the group to consider the following questions:

a. Would the people trust Zacchaeus from now on, or would they still hate him?

b. Would Zacchaeus still be a tax collector? If so, how would he behave in the future?

c. Would you trust someone who suddenly changed from cheating to honesty?

d. What have you learned from this incident that you will try to remember?

Draw the answers together at the end, and emphasize the tremendous change in Zacchaeus' life. The act of giving so much to the poor, and those he had deceived, was the clearest proof that Jesus had begun to change his life completely.

DIRECTOR'S TIPS

☞ When Zacchaeus comes back from meeting Jesus he should be very different. So at the start he could move slowly and keep a dead-pan face, then after his encounter he could come in running and grinning. You can probably think of other ideas, but make him very different (only don't change his clothes or Watt's joke will fall a bit flat!).

☞ For this sketch to work well Zacchaeus needs to be able to rattle off his complicated explanations quickly and without pausing. He should keep up a constant barrage of facts and figures to confuse Mr Watt.

☞ Make the name routine at the start slick with each of the performers saying their lines exactly on cue and without pausing.

An Eye for an Eye

STEVE — Dense, selfish, vicious.
CHRISTINE — Creepy, intelligent, malicious.
PAUL — Patient, humble, loving.

(*STEVE is loitering with intent to disembowel. Enter CHRISTINE. STEVE goes up to her threateningly.*)

STEVE: Oi creep!
CHRISTINE: Uh, excuse me, noddle bonce, but I am a prefect and if you so much as touch me I shall report you to the Head. All right?
STEVE: What? Oh no! I was only joking. Don't report me, honest I was only joking.
CHRISTINE: Yes, well ... I shall let you off this time, but just remember who's more important round here. (*CHRISTINE exits. Enter PAUL.*)
STEVE: Oi creep! Come 'ere and be thoroughly duffed up.
PAUL: Who me?
STEVE: Yeah. (*He starts to push PAUL around. PAUL doesn't retaliate.*) Had enough yet, weed? Or do you want me to carry on?
PAUL: If you want to ... yes.
STEVE: (*Confused beyond all capabilities*) What?
PAUL: If you really want to beat me up you might as well get on with it. I'm not going to start hitting you back.
STEVE: Eh what? Er, look stop mucking about. Do you want me to hit you or not?
PAUL: No, but if it would really make your day, then please get on with it. I'm late enough as it is.
STEVE: Aaargggh! Will you stop saying that? How can I hit you if you let me?
PAUL: Oh look, never mind. I'm sure there'll be someone along in a minute who'll put up a good fight.
STEVE: Yeah, I suppose so. (*STEVE walks off dejectedly. PAUL is about to go when CHRISTINE enters.*)
CHRISTINE: Ah sniveling one! There you are. Stop being a creep and carry my books to the end of the corridor. Come on quickly, you know the rules. I can ask anyone to carry my books down one corridor. And today, because I think you are an utter worm, I've chosen you. (*CHRISTINE gives PAUL an extremely heavy bag. She then marches off nagging at PAUL to keep up.*)
CHRISTINE: Right, here we are at the end of the corridor. Put them down there. Where's he got to? (*PAUL is still way behind.*) Oh come on. You can put them down now.
PAUL: It's OK. I'll take them to the lesson for you.
CHRISTINE: Why? What do you want? A merit?
PAUL: Well, not really. I was just offering to carry your books to the lesson.
CHRISTINE: Well, OK. (*She is obviously puzzled by this. They carry on until they get to the classroom. This is represented by three chairs and tables.*)
PAUL: There you go.
CHRISTINE: Uh, thank you .That's most, er, well, you know, sort of, um, kind of you. (*CHRISTINE looks very confused as they sit down. STEVE enters and sits down.*)
STEVE: Oi! Can I borrow a pen? Only I've forgotten mine.
CHRISTINE: Most certainly not. My daddy bought mine when he was in Paris. It cost £50 and is twenty two carat gold.
STEVE: I prefer writing with turnips. Get it? Turnips, carat. It's a joke.
CHRISTINE: Very nearly, thicky.
PAUL: Here, look! I've got one you can borrow. I'm afraid it's only from the newsagents and there's not a carrot in sight.
STEVE: Oh cheers, mate.
PAUL: Oh and I've got some tippex here. You can borrow that if you make any mistakes.
CHRISTINE: Mistakes? Ha, he can't even spell his name.
STEVE: Yes I can: H-I-S-N-A-M-E, get it? Another joke — that's three so far.
CHRISTINE: No, it's only two.
STEVE: Is it? (*Counts on his fingers looking confused. They write for a few moments.*)
PAUL: Right that's it, the end of the lesson. I've got to be going. (*He exits.*)
STEVE: Here, he's forgotten his pen.
CHRISTINE: You nicked it, you mean.
STEVE: No, I didn't. Not this one anyway. I couldn't nick something from him. He's sort of different.
CHRISTINE: Weird if you ask me. I mean what normal person offers to carry your books?
STEVE: Yeah and he didn't hit me back this morning.
CHRISTINE: Nor did I.
STEVE: That's 'cos you were going to report me to the Head. No, there's something different about him. I wonder what it is?

Revenge

TRAILER

Jesus told us to help our enemies, not hurt them. Who said Christianity was a soft option?

WORKSHOP

The young people will almost certainly argue that following what is taught here is impossible. We need to be sensitive to how hard it is for young people to understand and obey this teaching.

Read **Matthew 5:38-42**. Ask the group members what they think Jesus is saying. When someone says it's stupid, challenge them about the alternatives. Do this by asking what they would do if you hit them. When they say they would hit you back, say you would hit them harder. Keep on building this exchange, bringing in big brothers, boxers and eventually whole armies to hurt each other. When you get to all-out war, stop the argument and point out what has happened. By continually taking revenge, it has finally led to war.

'An eye for an eye' had originally been a limitation for revenge, but in Jesus' day it was being taught as the right way to take revenge. Instead of the law being seen as 'you can only take an eye for an eye' it was being read as 'you are *allowed* to take an eye for an eye'. The law had been saying you must limit your revenge by taking only what was taken from you. Jesus was saying you must limit your revenge to the extent of not taking revenge at all. A slap on the cheek (verse 39) was a public insult. In verse 41, Jesus is referring to the fact that a Roman soldier could make you carry his pack for him, but only for one kilometre. Make the point that Jesus is saying we need to love the person who is hurting us, and by our actions we are trying to win them for Christ. It is more important to love the person than to take revenge. Encourage the young people to come up with ideas of how we can go the extra mile today, and how we can learn to 'turn the other cheek'.

DIRECTOR'S TIPS

☞ Make all the characters really different. Steve must be really dense and thuggish, Christine needs to be obviously malicious and sneaky, whereas Paul should be down to earth. Make the differences greater by having suggestions of costume — ties, hats, glasses ...

☞ When Christine makes Paul carry her books, they could walk right round the room. This would give time for the three chairs and tables to be set up.

☞ Set up the chairs in a straight row at an angle to the audience. This enables the performers to look at each other without being in profile, or having their backs to the audience.

All or Nothing

MYRCLUNCKSKY — A gangster.
MALONE — An American policeman.
DIBBLE — Another American policeman.

(*MALONE and DIBBLE have arrested MYRCLUNCKSKY and are now interrogating him. MYRCLUNCKSKY is seated at a table.*)

DIBBLE: OK, Myrclunksky, are you going to talk, or do we have to force it out of you?

MYRCLUNCKSKY: I'll talk.

DIBBLE: (*Obviously disappointed*) Oh, are you sure? We're very good at forcing it out of you. The bruises hardly show at all.

MALONE: What are you on about, Dibble?

DIBBLE: Interrogation, sir! Breaking Myclunksky's will, legs, nose and back to force him to give us the names of the other members of his gang.

MALONE: Look, this isn't some second-rate gangster film, you know. We'll question him in a civilized manner. We'll use our powers of careful persuasion to draw the truth out, and then we'll use our cunning and guile to trick him into revealing who the other culprits are.

DIBBLE: Couldn't we just hit him?

MALONE: No! Now you take the notes while I do the talking. Now Myrclunksky, how about you tell us who else was involved in this ice-cream racket?

MYRCLUNCKSKY: Never! I will never betray the rest of the gang.

MALONE: Now look, we're going to break this ice-cream racket even if it takes till tea time. So why not make it easy on yourself and tell us who else is involved?

DIBBLE: Yeah, who else is involved in this stinking outfit? Stealing ice-creams from babies and then re-selling them. That's really low, Myrclunksky, it's really sick. Why, if I wasn't such a kind person I'd go for you myself. (*DIBBLE acts out this next part, getting really worked up and shouting.*) I'd grab you round the throat and I'd shake and shake and shake until you promise never to steal another ice-cream again.

MALONE: Yes, thank you Dibble, very noble. Now will you please leave Myrclunksky alone before we get done for police brutality.

DIBBLE: (*Suddenly realising what he's done.*) Er yeah, sorry sir.

MALONE: Now come on, Myrclunksky. Just the names of the guys and then we can all go and have a nice cup of tea.

MYRCLUNCKSKY: OK, I'll give you the names of the little guys, the ones who aren't important. But I'll never split on Knuckles. Whoops!

MALONE: Knuckles, eh? I had a hunch he might be behind this. Well, come on. Who else?

MYRCLUNCKSKY: Well, there's Tiny, Batty, Fingers and the one we call Spong.

DIBBLE: Why do you call him that?

MYRCLUNCKSKY: It's his name.

MALONE: And who else? We've got to have all the names.

MYRCLUNCKSKY: Look, I've told you enough. Now how about you let me go?

MALONE: Never, not until every one of those crooks is captured. While they're out there no child with an ice-cream is safe. All the time there is just one of those low-down thieving varmints on the loose...I'm going to carry on with this sketch!

MYRCLUNCKSKY: No, please. No! You didn't tell me you were going to be that cruel. But if that's the way you want it. The main leaders are Squash Face, Doberman and Sue.

MALONE: OK, Dibble, we've got them now. Let's go and round them up. Oh and give Myrclunksky an ice-cream. There's some in the freezer I got cheap yesterday from my mate Spong. (*Pause*)
(*MALONE looks panic-stricken at the implication of what he's said.*) Ahhh!

© CPAS 1994

Persecution

TRAILER

When God knows all that we do, why do we try and keep things from him?

WORKSHOP

Ask the group about the last time they said sorry to God. **Psalm 32** gives a clear account of how we need to have our sins forgiven. **Psalm 32: 3,4** are David's vivid description of the state he was in before he confessed his sins. However, in verse 5 David describes how he owned up to God and how God forgave all of his sins. To avoid being in the situation David describes in verses 3 and 4 we need to confess all our sins.

Just as there was no point in Myrcluncksky only giving the names of a few people, there's no point in us asking forgiveness for some of our sins, the really bad ones or the ones we don't feel guilty about! We need to ask forgiveness for all of them, even the ones we don't know about or have forgotten. The great promise in verse 5b, however, is that God will always forgive all of our sins.

DIRECTOR'S TIPS

☞ During the sketch you can add as many American cop show clichés as possible. Feel free to add any references to the FBI, Feds, the DA's office and only having forty eight hours to solve the case otherwise the CIA will be called in!

☞ For the interrogation, sit Myrclucksky behind a desk with a reading lamp on it. This can then be shone directly onto his face.

☞ Dibble and Malone should be constantly adjusting their ties and drinking coffee out of paper cups!

43

The Exhibition

SENOR ENTREES — A famous Spanish painter.

DIANNE — A visitor to the gallery.

(The scene is an art gallery. There are paintings on the walls. In the middle of the collection are two pictures of a man, painted in blue and labelled 'Peter'. There is also a picture of a dress. These all need to be done on plain postcards. The great Spanish artist SENOR ENTREES is looking at the pictures. Enter DIANNE. She looks at all the pictures and then spots SENOR ENTREES.)

DIANNE: Er, excuse me sir, but are you him?

ENTREES: Que? *(That little question that Manuel in 'Fawlty Towers' was always asking.)*

DIANNE: Are you him? Senor Entrees, the world-famous Spanish artist, known the world over for the series of pictures entitled *Studies of a Sewerage Pipe*?

ENTREES: Si!

DIANNE: Sea? No, it was definitely a sewerage pipe!

ENTREES: No. Not *sea* – si! It's Spanish for yes. Yes, I am Senor Entrees, the world-famous Spanish artist, known the world over for the series of pictures entitled *Studies of a Sewerage Pipe*.

DIANNE: Oh wow! This is a great honour for me, Senor. I've been a fan of yours for years. In fact ever since I first saw your series of pictures entitled *Studies of a Sewerage Pipe*. I mean, your studies of the pipe, the light and the atmosphere were quite spectacular. You truly mastered your subject. They were certainly much better than these amateur efforts. *(She motions to the pictures on the wall.)* And they are all so small, especially these two stupid ones here, both called 'Peter' and this load of old tosh entitled *A Dress*. Nothing here compares with the skill and mastery of your art. I'm surprised you can bear to see such rubbish.

ENTREES: Actually, I painted these.

DIANNE: Ha ha! What, when you were five, Senor? Good joke that — you painting a load of old junk like these. These really are pathetic. I can't believe anyone would paint two people in blue. They look really stupid. *(She has a closer look. ENTREES is beginning to look offended.)* Look, they're even done on postcards. How idiotic! If I ever painted things like these I'd throw them away. And this one of the dress is so unrealistic. It's a disgrace to have it on show.

ENTREES: But I did paint them! They are self-portraits done during my blue period.

DIANNE: Get away! You're a classic artist. No-one will ever better your *Studies of a Sewerage Pipe*. You're a natural genius. *(ENTREES is looking very offended.)* DIANNE: *(Suddenly feeling rather stupid)* Is your name really Peter?

ENTREES: It is. And those are my finest pictures. Two self portraits in blue on postcards, and this one *(points to the dress)* is my mother's favourite dress.

DIANNE: *(The light suddenly dawning)* What, you mean?

ENTREES: Yes!

BOTH: *(They deliver this line like a joke in a pantomime and point to each thing as they name it.)* Senor Entrees, on a postcard, two blue Peters, a dress!

Criticism

This whole sketch is incredibly contrived to get you to the punch line! When you say it, it should sound like **'Send your entries on a postcard to Blue Peter's address'** — hence the joke! Make sure that only those people in the sketch know the punch line. The punch line has nothing to do with the lesson behind the sketch, so don't try to draw any theological point from it!

TRAILER

When you say a person is rubbish, who are you criticising? That person, or the one who made that person?

WORKSHOP

In the sketch Dianne was praising the artist, yet she said his work was rubbish. Obviously this can't be done. If you say the artist's work is rubbish, you are saying that he is a rubbish artist.

Read **James 3:9-12**. Here James is saying that we can't praise God and curse people. If we curse or say people are rubbish we are calling God who made them rubbish. You could tie this into **1 John 4:20-21**. If we call our fellow-Christians, who are created in God's image, rubbish, how can we claim to love God? To love the creator involves loving his creation.

DIRECTOR'S TIPS

☞ Create as good an art gallery as possible. If you have a handy wall nearby, stick some pictures to it. If you don't have a wall try using a table standing on its end.

☞ The pictures can be of anything and of any quality, but the more the better. Use pictures cut out of magazines as well as any original masterpieces you have lying around at home!

Other resources from Pathfinders

Throughout this book there have been references to other publications where the sketches were first published, mainly *Compass*. On the next two pages there is some information about resources available from Pathfinders.

Compass

Compass is the Pathfinder teaching resource for use with the 11-14+ age group. It is a three year syllabus, with enough material for forty sessions per year. Each year ten major topic areas are covered, with four sessions on each of the following subjects:

1) The Bible — Just another book?
2) God — Lord of All.
3) Church — Place of belonging.
4) Home — Where it all counts.
5) Salvation — God's rescue plan.
6) Jesus — In a class of His own.
7) Mission — Telling others.
8) Future — In safe hands.
9) Prayer — Two way contact.
10) Holy Spirit — Closest friend.

Each A4 format book contains two teaching units with more than enough material for eight sessions. The material seeks to involve the young people in activity, which will help them to remember and understand. The teaching content is Bible-based and encourages the young people to learn scripture. The teaching story-lines are backed by illustrations which are copyright-free, allowing you to reproduce them for the group. See page 47 for the complete *Compass* syllabus.

Growing More Like Jesus

For use with the 13-18 age group, it offers a basic nurture course using Luke's Gospel. It is designed to strengthen a group's identity and provide leadership training.

Assembly Line

Twenty complete school assemblies for anyone to use with pupils in the first three years of secondary education. Each one takes a Bible character and presents the message in a way that is suitable and relevant for assemblies. Suggestions and ideas are given on a range of topics to help make assemblies appeal to young teenagers. Permission to photocopy is granted for all the relevant material such as cartoons and drama sketches.

Bible Based Resources for Youth Groups

A series of practical books designed to enable truths in the Bible to be taught faithfully and enjoyably with copyright-free pages.

All Together Forever explores Ephesians in a challenging and refreshing way over ten sessions. Some of the topics covered include: the will of God, the Church, the Devil and the armour of God.

Pressure Points looks at issues facing young people today: drugs, alcohol, poverty, racism, sexuality, materialism... . Ten sessions all based on the Bible to help your group get to grips with these important areas.

Harping On? A 'ready to use' resource on the Psalms, for youth groups which studies six of the better known Psalms. It is designed so that each session can be used by itself as a one-off, although it could also be taught as a series of studies.

To order, or for more information about these and other resources from CPAS contact:
CPAS sales on (0926) 334242, or 24 hour ansaphone service on (0926) 335855.

The Compass Syllabus

Book One: Units 1 & 2
1. An explanation of how to understand, trust, learn and obey what the Bible teaches.
2. God is our creator who keeps His promises, provides for us and knows us inside out.

Book Two: Units 3 & 4
3. The Church is a place of belonging for His saints and His children. He calls us into action.
4. The Home is where faith must be seen in action. How can you survive with parents?!

Book Three: Units 5 & 6
5. God's rescue plan tackles the problem of sin and gives something to look forward to.
6. Jesus the great teacher and giver of life, as seen in Mark's gospel.

Book Four: Units 7 & 8
7. Mission is all about telling others. This unit will help the young people share their faith.
8. The Future is safe for the Christian, but how does God guide us?

Book Five: Units 9 & 10
9. How does prayer work and what can get in the way? It is our two-way contact with God
10. The Holy Spirit is the Christian's closest friend. His job is to make us more like Jesus.

Book Six: Units 11 & 12
11. This unit focuses on parts of Psalm 119, and what it teaches us about God's word.
12. God's close encounters with Noah, Jonah, Moses and Daniel, and what we can learn.

Book Seven: Units 13 & 14
13. Paul's letter to the Ephesians shows us the worth of the church, and why we belong.
14. The sermon on the mount is full of practical tips on Christian living.

Book Eight: Units 15 & 16
15. Jesus' encounters with Peter, Simon the Pharisee, Zacchaeus and a rich young man.
16. The "I am" sayings in John give us a great insight as to why Jesus is in a class of His own.

Book Nine: Units 17 & 18
17. Paul's second missionary journey is fun to follow and helps us to share our faith.
18. Paul told the Christians at Thessalonica about what will happen when Jesus returns.

Book Ten: Units 19 & 20
19. Jesus taught His disciples "The Lord's Prayer". What makes it so special?
20. What are the fruits of the Holy Spirit and how can we cultivate them in our lives?

Book Eleven: Units 21 & 22
21. Why are there four gospels? What's so special about Matthew, Mark and Luke?
22. John's gospel helps us see how God is creator, and yet we can call Him "Father".

Book Twelve: Units 23 & 24
23. Where did the church come from and how did it spread? A look at Acts.
24. James has a lot to say about the tongue in his letter. Very relevant for leaders too!

Book Thirteen: Units 25 & 26
25. The Easter events - were they planned, or was it just a tragedy? God's Rescue plan.
26. What do Jesus' titles Messiah, Son of God, Lord, and Son of Man really mean?

Book Fourteen: Units 27 & 28
27. A focus on overseas mission, and what we can learn about sharing your faith.
28. What hope did Peter give for the future to those Christians suffering for their faith?

Book Fifteen: Units 29 & 30
29. An in-depth look at prayer, with practical help on praying in group sessions.
30. How does the Holy Spirit help us grow as individuals, and as a church?

Bible Index

Reference	Page	Title	Theme
Exodus 3:13,14	34	Beyond the Game	The nature of God.
2 Samuel 6:12-23	20	Playing Tonight	Worship.
Psalm 32	42	All or Nothing	Confession.
Psalm 51	22	It's a Fair Cop	Sin and forgiveness.
Isaiah 55:8,9	34	Beyond the Game	The nature of God.
Matthew 5:38-42	40	An Eye for an Eye	Revenge.
Matthew 7:21	6	The Usurper	Who is Jesus?
Matthew 7:24-27	28	Lord Wormington Squirrel and his Faithful Butler, Boote	Obedience.
Matthew 12:15-21	24	The Kept Promise	God's promises.
Matthew 28:11-15	18	Caiaphas's Catastrophic Caper	The Resurrection.
Luke 7:41-42	16	The Debtors	Forgiveness.
Luke 12:15-21	30	Empty-handed	Death.
Luke 17:11-19	10	The Assembly	Prejudice.
Luke 19:1-10	38	All Change	Zacchaeus.
Luke 22:42	32	Innocent	Why did Jesus die?
Luke 23:13-25	32	Innocent	Why did Jesus die?
John 14:6	12	Ridiculous Routes	The uniqueness of Christ.
John 20:24-31	18	Caiaphas's Catastrophic Caper	The Resurrection.
Acts 5 & 8	26	What Would You do?	Persecution.
Acts 16:16-34	8	The Pet	Witnessing.
Acts 5:33-39	18	Caiaphas's Catastrophic Caper	The Resurrection.
James 3:9-12	44	The Exhibition	Criticism.
James 5:19	14	Spot the Brain Cell	Lying.
1 Peter 1:13-2:12	36	Be Prepared	Holy living.
1 John 4:20-21	44	The Exhibition	Criticism.